A Tale of Pudicho's People

Cashinahua Accounts of European Contact

**SIL International and
The International Museum of Cultures
Publications in Ethnography**

Publication 38

Publications in Ethnography (formerly International Museum of Cultures Series) is a series published jointly by SIL International and the International Museum of Cultures. The series focuses on cultural studies of minority peoples of various parts of the world. While most volumes are authored by members of SIL International, suitable works by others will also occasionally form part of the series.

Series Editors

Barbara Moore
David Wakefield

Volume Editor

Marilyn Mayers

Production Staff

Bonnie Brown, Managing Editor
Karoline Fisher, Compositor
Hazel Shorey, Graphic Artist

A Tale of Pudicho's People

Cashinahua Accounts of European Contact

Richard Montag

A Publication of
SIL International and
The International Museum of Cultures
Dallas, Texas

© 2002 SIL International
Library of Congress Catalog No: 2002092333
ISBN: 1-55671-131-X
ISSN: 0-0895-9897

Printed in the United States of America

All Rights Reserved

06 05 04 03 02   7 6 5 4 3 2 1

No part of this publication may be reproduced, stored in a retrieval system, or transmitted in any form or by any means—electronic, mechanical, photocopy, recording, or otherwise—without the express permission of SIL International, with the exception of brief excerpts in journal articles or reviews.

Copies of this and other publications of SIL International may be obtained from

International Academic Bookstore
SIL International
7500 W. Camp Wisdom Road
Dallas, TX 75236-5699

Voice: 972-708-7404
Fax: 972-708-7363
Email: academic_books@sil.org
Internet: http://www.ethnologue.com

Dedication

I dedicate this work to the loving memory of Mr. John McIlhenny of Baton Rouge, Louisiana, with sincere thanks for his encouragement and support at many phases of the effort that went into this study. He was one of the few to visit the Cashinahua in Balta and often spoke of that trip and his Cashinahua friends over the years.

Contents

Dedication	v
Acknowledgments	ix
1 Introduction	1
2 Initial Contact	11
3 The Escape	27
4 Return to the Old Ways	37
5 Renewing Contact with Outsiders	51
6 An Unequal Situation	65
7 Different Outsiders	77
8 Replacements	99
9 Accelerated Change	117
10 The Present-Day Situation	137
Appendix	165
References	167

Acknowledgments

This historical-ethnographic study has not been the product of my efforts alone. Much of it comes from my personal experiences with the Cashinahua, but those experiences could not have come to fruition without help. Special thanks go to our Cashinahua friends who suffered with my wife and me as we learned their language. I give special acknowledgment to Pudicho, who told me many stories and who has joined his ancestors at a ripe old age. Pudicho's son, Grompes, and his nephew, Mario, did their best to direct me in the ways of Cashinahua culture. Marcelino Pinedo labored over the years to help me pronounce their words correctly and would not let me make mistakes. I count these three men as special friends and was greatly saddened to receive word that Grompes died an early death in 1999.

This book comes directly from my Ph.D. dissertation and I wish to acknowledge my committee members at the University of Albany—Dr. Gary Gossen, Dr. Aaron Broadwell, and Dr. Louise Burkhart—whose probing questions helped me sharpen the focus of my dissertation. In the beginning, Dr. Robert Cromack's dissertation on Cashinahua discourse became a great help after we learned enough of the language to understand it. Also during the dissertation process Dr. Kenneth Kensinger, who also worked with the Cashinahua, was a continual help, giving advice and criticism when necessary. Also many thanks to Nina Moss for her literary and editorial help with the original manuscript.

Last but not least, extra special thanks to my helpmate, Susan, who was at my side all the years we worked in Peru and has been my sounding board as we labored together to recall old happenings.

1
Introduction

Pudicho's people, the Cashinahua, are a self-identifying ethnic group who now live on various rivers and streams at the headwaters of the Juruá and Purús rivers in Brazil and Peru. They have retained their own language but increasingly speak the national language with outsiders as needed. They call themselves *juni kuin*[1] 'True', 'Real', or 'Genuine Man', but recognize the outsider designation of "Cashinahua". However, they do not use this name except when speaking Spanish or Portuguese.

This study relates the experiences of one Cashinahua group who migrated to Peru sometime in the early years of the twentieth century to escape the turmoil of the rubber boom era. Further, it details their changing perspectives as they increased their contact with the outside world beginning in the mid-1940s. The English historian John Hemming wrote about the invasion by rubber collectors of the southernmost headwaters of the Juruá and Purús rivers toward the close of the nineteenth century. He said, "During these turbulent years, many uncontacted tribes clashed with rubber men. But both sides in these skirmishes and massacres were illiterate, so we know almost nothing of the history of the Indians of those distant forests" (Hemming 1987:279). However, the Cashinahua of Peru have remembered what happened to their parents and grandparents in Brazil. These memories, plus their own experiences, help shape their changing attitudes as they continue to interface with the larger world around them.

---

[1]Any Cashinahua words that are given are pronounced like Spanish except for the following: (1) the letter *n* when it is not followed by a vowel indicates nasalization on the previous vowel, (2) the letter *v* is pronounced as English w, (3) x is similar to the English *sh*, and (4) the letter *e* is the close central unrounded vowel as in the second syllable of roses.

My wife, Susan Montag, and I began living and working with the Cashinahua of Peru in June of 1969 with three purposes: (1) linguistics—to learn their language and continue the process of putting it into a usable written form; (2) literacy—to provide simple primers for teaching reading and to initiate a reading program; and (3) translation—to begin to translate the Bible in their language. Fortunately, we had the opportunity to begin work with them in a predominantly monolingual situation. Even though we communicated in their language almost from the beginning, however, they did not have enough confidence in me to tell me their personal histories or intimate folklore until we had been with them for six years. By then we had become knowledgeable, semi-accepted outsiders.

After several months, I began recording stories told by Pudicho, the retired headman, in order to help me in my linguistic studies. I continued, as time permitted, to record his stories for approximately eight years as an aid to my cultural understanding. When Pudicho told me stories, we were usually at my house in Balta, and he knew he was speaking to me and to the tape recorder. He generally spoke without animation or gestures. It seemed to me that he had an endless supply of stories. Sometimes he chose the topic, and at other times he asked what I wanted to hear about. I did not initially have enough knowledge to choose a topic, but in 1975 I asked him what life was like for him when he was a child. It was then that he surprised me with the long narrative that is the core of this work.

The situation was similar with the other older men when I asked them to tell me about their childhood and lifetime experiences. They knew they were speaking to me and the tape recorder and that I was in the habit of reviewing the tapes with the younger men—their sons, nephews, and grandsons, who were my regular language helpers. All of the personal histories, descriptions, and legends contained in this study are classified by the Cashinahua as *miyui* 'telling something'.

To better understand the following narratives, a small amount of geographical and historical data is necessary. Prior to the coming of the Europeans, the ancestors of the Cashinahua of Peru lived in the far western headwaters of various southern tributaries of the Juruá River and over onto streams which drain into the Purús River to the south (see map 1).

At that time, all of the indigenous peoples of the Amazonian lowlands were either river Indians or foot Indians. The river Indians mastered the art of canoe making and lived off the richer floodplains of the major rivers and their tributaries. But they did not have a major food crop that they could grow on the richer soils of the floodplains during the dry season until maize was brought from Central America. The manioc which needed more time to mature was grown on hillsides to avoid the floods of the rainy season.

The foot Indians lived up away from the major rivers and traveled only by trails, wading across the larger streams during the dry season. Their upland areas were not as rich in fauna as the floodplains occupied by the river Indians, but they had a larger area between the rivers in which to hunt and forage. Their gardens would have had the same manioc, sweet potatoes, peanuts, and native flat beans as the river Indians, but because of the dispersion of their resources the foot Indians had to move their villages more often than the river Indians. The coming of maize gave all a stable, storable crop which made larger population concentrations more possible.

Map 1. The Alto Purús Region

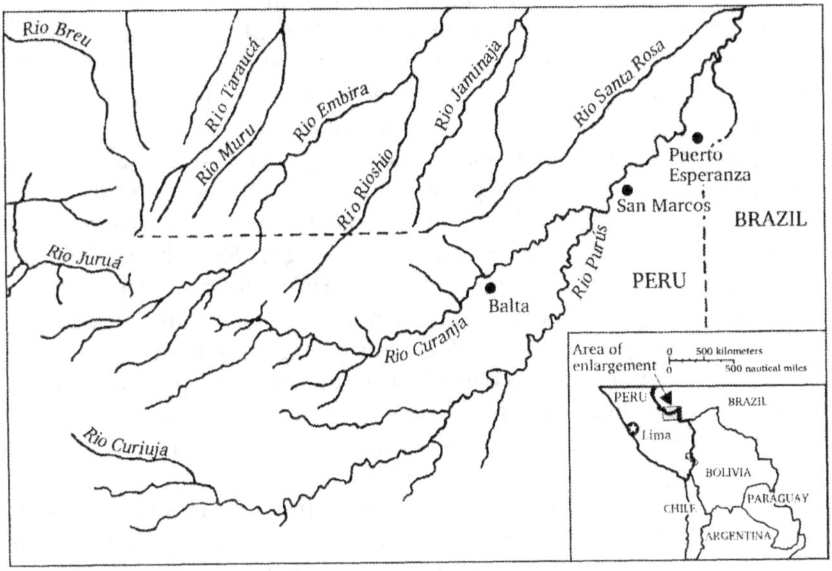

The Cashinahua of Peru told me that their ancestors had always lived up away from the large rivers and did not learn canoe use or making until they descended to live by the navigable streams in Peru. They also told me that their people had always lived interspersed with people who spoke like the Arawakans. They told of some raiding but mostly of peaceful times. There was never a shortage of territory, only the need to move around in order to have enough space for themselves.

It is difficult to determine the exact date when the Cashinahua's ancestors first heard about the appearance of light-skinned outsiders with firearms. Word may have come up the Juruá or over from the Ucayali Valley. Chandless reported that one group at the headwater of the Purús River had contact with Catholic missionaries on the Ucayali (Chandless 1867:100–101). If this was the case for the Purús in the last century, word could easily have reached the Juruá region early by the same route. If this knowledge did not reach the headwaters of the Juruá River in the 1500s with the coming of the Spanish to the Ucayali Valley, it was positively known by the mid-1700s. After 1677 the Portuguese settlers on the Amazon, upriver from the mouth of the Negro River, were capturing their labor supply from the indigenous people on the Juruá River. By 1775 the official records have Catuquinas and Yochinauas listed in the labor force (Tastevin 1943:1). This shows that expeditions foraging for cocoa, cloves, sarsaparilla, and Brazil nuts had penetrated far up the Juruá River, because Catuquina is the name of an existing Panoan group in that area, and Yochinaua is a Panoan word which means "Spirit People". If these Panoan people were being taken as forced laborers, news of this and the presence of fire arms would certainly have been passed upriver.

The use of indigenous labor by the Europeans has been an operating principle since the first Portuguese contact in 1500. Those early years set the basic attitudes towards the indigenous peoples which were in effect when the Cashinahua were contacted in the Juruá River basin. The tenets of this attitude were: (1) indigenous territory should be taken over for the national good, (2) indigenous labor should by some means be acquired in order to promote the national economy, and (3) indigenous women should be used to produce a halfbreed population more receptive to acculturation. The indigenous people were always seen as a labor force to be used to tame the forests for the good of the settlers. To fulfill these goals the national policy was to "descend" all native groups to live in contact with Brazilian society and be part of the national economy. The general policy of "descending" these groups to live in controled circumstances was initiated by the Jesuits in 1553. The people were "reduced", i.e., gathered to live in orderly mission settlements, so that the priests and brothers could better instruct them, acculturate them to European ways, and make them available to work for a fair wage. At first they had success with the indigenous groups who were already defeated, demoralized, and seeking protection from settlers. The goal of the Jesuits was to replace the indigenous cultures by acculturation. When there was resistance, the Jesuits decided that such people were inherently an inferior race. The things the Jesuits tried to teach them were foreign to their environment and

Introduction

deprived them of their indigenous skills without equipping them to compete (Hemming 1978:104–107, 116).[2]

By 1650 the Spanish realized that they did not have sufficient resources to control both coasts of South America and keep the Portuguese in check. So they recognized the boundaries of the Viceroyalty of Peru as indicated in map 2 (adapted from Williamson 1992). They ceded to Portugal the eastern coast from the mouth of the Amazon River to what is now Montevideo and by default the lower section of the Amazon. By the late 1600s the Spanish were still doing very little to establish their claim to the section of the great river upstream from the Rio Negro, and the Portuguese wanted to claim it by right of exploration and conquest. What followed was a political and military tug-of-war between the reinforced Spanish Jesuits and the Portuguese Carmelites, with the indigenous peoples as pawns. And because the Portuguese provided more consistent military backing to the Carmelites than the Spanish authorities in Quito did for the Jesuits, the Portuguese prevailed. The issue was officially settled in 1750 by the Treaty of Madrid, with the Portuguese getting the main river (Amazon) up to the mouth of the Javari (Yavari) River and thus the best access to the vast majority of the Amazon basin (Hemming 1978:430–434).

When the treaty dividing the Amazon basin was made, there was nothing worth fighting over in the far western rain forests. However, a century later the importance of rubber radically changed the situation. In the intervening years much happened politically in Spanish America. After the colonies won their independence from Spain, greater Peru, including what is now Bolivia, claimed all the territory south of the demarcation line, east as far as the Madeira River. Then in 1826 the people of La Paz decided that they wanted to be out from under the historical control of Lima and separated themselves from Peru, taking the name Bolivia. They claimed the territory of the previous greater Peru which lay north of the territory historically administered from La Paz, including the headwaters of the Juruá River where the ancestors of the Cashinahua were then living (see map 3).

---

[2]The example set by the Jesuits has been followed to a greater or lesser degree by secular authorities and by other missionaries to this day. European and North American missionaries, both Roman Catholic and Protestant, have often mistakenly considered dark-skinned peoples around the world to be child-like and in need of outward change. In order for them to change spiritually, they must conform to Western standards (Dirks 1992:16, Beidleman 1982:128, Comaroff 1992:144–145). My wife and I reject this position, although we soon discovered that, for both the average Peruvian and the government officials with whom we dealt, it was axiomatic that all the indigenous peoples within their territory would eventually conform to the national culture.

Map 2. Viceroyalty of Peru

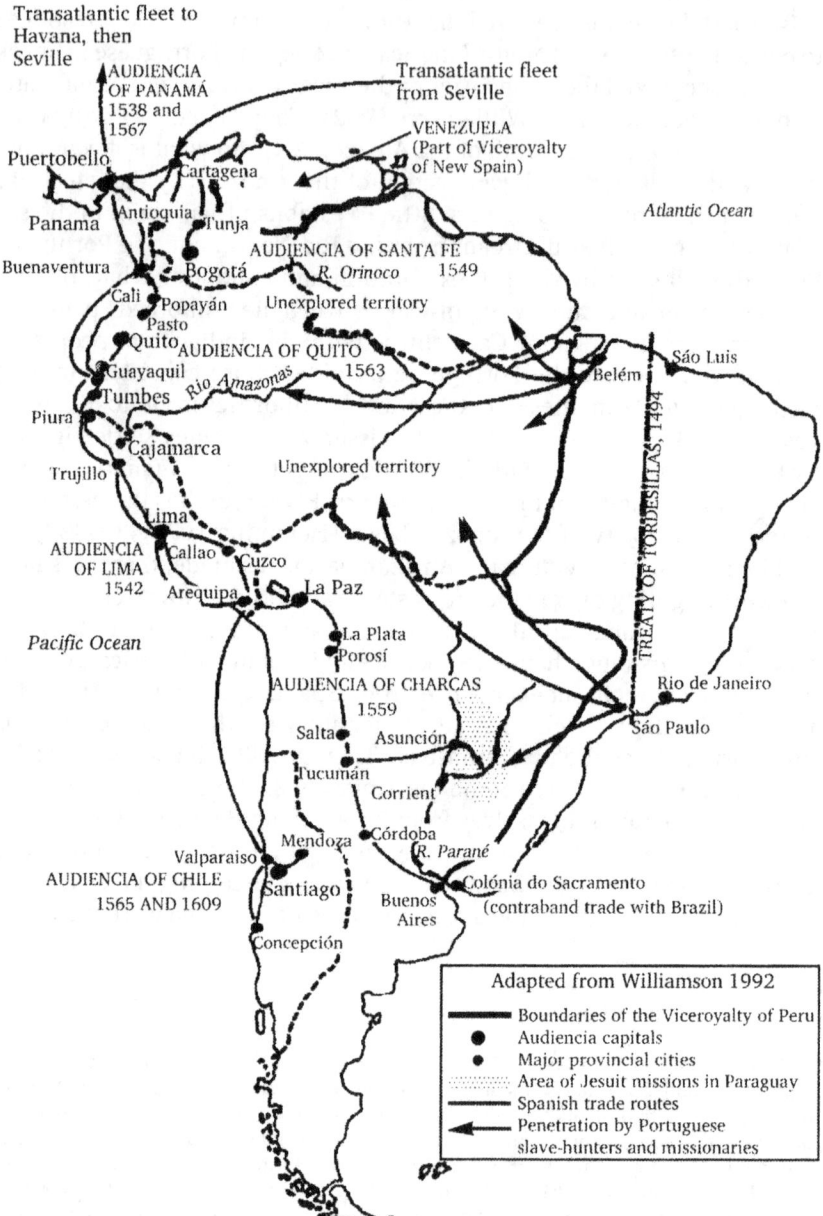

Map 3. Spanish South America

Then as the price of rubber rose, more and more men and a few women poured into far western Amazonia at the headwaters of the Juruá and Purús rivers. The entire area became known as Acre, after the Acre River, whose drainage was richer in rubber trees than other parts of Amazonia. Most of these new inhabitants considered themselves Brazilian and resented paying taxes to Bolivian officials so they formed a nearly independent republic and rebelled in 1899 and 1902. When Brazil learned that Bolivia was seeking a foreign group to control the area as a rubber concession, they intervened militarily, purchasing Acre from Bolivia for two million British pounds (Hemming 1987:278–279). This occasioned the stationing of Captain Luiz Sombra in that area; some of his account is included in a later chapter.

It was during those turbulent times that the great grandparents and grandparents of the Cashinahua, who now live in Peru, first came into contact with the outside world. They later severed that contact to escape mistreatment. The exodus of the rubber collectors after 1913, when the world price for rubber began to fall, provided the Cashinahua with unoccupied territory in which to seclude themselves until the 1940s.

The remainder of this book is a series of texts starting with the long narrative of the retired headman, Pudicho (set in block quotes). It demonstrates his steadfastness in seeking recontact with the outside world in order to again have things such as clothing, tools, soap, and beads. Pudicho's narrative is bolstered by the remembrances of his two younger brothers, Idiodoro and Belisario, and his cousins, Nacimiento and Araguana (set in block quotes). All of these relatives grew to manhood without contact with the outside world.[3]

At intervals I provide comments in order to help the reader to understand some unspoken cultural or contextual information such as transitions within or between various voices. The purpose of my commentary and the selection of texts is to demonstrate that the Cashinahua were, and are, both active and reactive in their contact with the outside world. My wife and I participated in and witnessed some of the major events in their lives over the past thirty years. I have been very fortunate to have had good transcription help from the younger generation and translation help from some of the narrators or their sons. However, because I was collector, translator, and the one who selected which texts to present, I am somewhat intrusive in the text, even when dealing with the time periods before we entered their lives. I attempted to leave my voice in the background but the many hours, days, and years of digging out the meanings

---

[3]Much of the translated text is kept quite literal and will sound unnatural in English in the adverbs that show continuation or repetition of activities, adverbs which we do not usually include in English texts.

Introduction

of these narratives became part of my life and it shows through. I cannot escape it; I am as much a participant as anyone in the text.

As I seek to explain the Cashinahua's culture, this multivocal history is also an ethnography, guided by the topics that arise in the narratives. I bring my voice more to the fore at the moment when my wife and I enter their story and were drawn into their lives as advocates for health, education, and community welfare. The narratives by Pudicho's son, Grompes, and his nephews, Mario and Joaquin (also in block quotes), speak directly to these issues and continue the story until 1994.

Also, in order to provide a larger context I include, where appropriate, texts by outsiders, such as John Hemming, an historian who is the main source of the historical context; Luiz Sombra, a Brazilian Army officer, and Constant Tastevin, a Roman Catholic priest, both of whom worked in the area where some of the early incidents occurred; Harald Schultz, a German photographer who visited the Cashinahua in Peru in 1951; Dini Fulano, a river trader who made the first permanent contact with the Cashinahua in Peru; and Kenneth Kensinger who was the first linguist to study their language (also in block quotes). These additional voices are quoted extensively as are other Cashinahua voices so that the reader will have enough of the quoted context to understand how it fits in with Pudicho's larger story.

The following chapters reveal the unfolding perspective and culture of an indigenous group who escaped the ravages of contact by threading a seam between two colonially influenced powers. The chapters present the narrative chronologically, beginning with the initial contact in chapter 2 and continuing the story from the escape to the present time in chapters 3 through 10. As events, cultural practices, and various contexts are presented, the reader is encouraged to visualize a world few outsiders have had the opportunity to experience.

2

Initial Contact

At some time in the 1880s or early 1890s, when the world demand for rubber was increasing and rubber tappers were pushing to the extremities of the Juruá River basin, one indigenous man said to another:[4]

1. "Make contact with one of the roofed canoes of the outsiders, the kind with motors. After you make contact, get me some spoons and large fishhooks. I will make a spoon into a nose ornament for myself and we can use the hooks to catch large fish for everyone. Get them for me; you're the brave one, aren't you?" The other (First Shot) replied, "Yes, I am brave and I am also fierce."

Then the first one replied, "I know you are brave because you always make your wife listen to you. If you contact the outsiders, the ones who come in the canoes with roofs, I will always consider you to be a fierce one. Listen, maybe a motor is coming now."

2. The other replied, "Is that so? Maybe I should do it. Okay, I'll make contact with them for you." After saying this, he put on his ceremonial decorations. He put on new cotton leg bands; he put on new cotton wrist bands; he inserted mother-of-pearl disks in large holes in his ear lobes; he put on a headdress made of oriole tail feathers with macaw tail feathers standing up in back; then he inserted pompoms,

---

[4]The text blocks told to me by Pudicho are numbered for easy cross-referencing. Other text blocks are from someone other than Pudicho.

made from immature palm fronds, to hang from his waistband and from his upper arm bands, and stood there decked out in his ceremonial attire.

3. Then upon seeing First Shot so decorated, other Yaminahuas began saying, "Wow, you really are a fierce one! Truly, you are a fierce one! We also realize that you are truly brave. So let the boat come!" and so the boat came long ago, so I was told.

4. A boat with a motor was coming, "Tiki, tiki, tiki." As it came up the nearby straight stretch, First Shot asked, "What shall I say?" They said, "If you call out 'Papa! Papa!' they will see you and stop."

To get their attention, he stepped out onto the open river bank and called out, "*Minu mine xada,* 'I am good, I am good.' *Aimi xada,* 'You also are good, you also are good.' Come! Come! Bring your boat. Bring your boat. Bring your canoe over here."

5. Slowly the canoe turned around and while it was approaching the bank, the ones who were hidden in the undergrowth were suffering diarrhea out of fear, causing quite an odor. As the boat nosed into the bank, First Shot jumped and climbed on board and was led into the enclosed area.

6. Those who were in the jungle continued to have diarrhea and kept thinking out loud, "Maybe they are killing him; maybe they are doing him in." As they waited, First Shot said to the crew, "Give me spoons. Give me spoons. I want spoons." They gave him some spoons, some large fishhooks, and some matches. And after sending him back to shore in a peaceful manner, they resumed their journey upriver to get the rubber that the collectors had stockpiled months before and which was waiting for them. Thinking of those upriver, they had given First Shot what he requested and were leaving.

7. Then as the boat disappeared, the Yaminahuas came out on the river bank and said, "First Shot, you are truly very brave. Because you have made contact with outsiders we are able to fear and respect you. You are really brave."

> Saying, "I got them for you," First Shot divided the fishhooks, spoons, and matches among those who were with him. After having received those things, they all came home. This is how my people report First Shot's peaceful contact with the outsiders, and how he later got contact with them, so I was told.[5]

This is a brief story that Pudicho's group has adopted as part of their history, a story concerning a brave indigenous man named First Shot. This contact influenced Pudicho's father's group who, like First Shot's group, lived away from the navigable rivers to peacefully accept the approach of other outsiders. When the rubber tappers first came, contact with them was easy to avoid because the rubber trees that the outsiders sought grew on the flood plains and were tapped only during the dry season, and the early tappers did not set up year-round residences. First Shot was not a Cashinahua, but was of another Panoan-speaking group, a Yaminahua, a term the Cashinahua use to refer to any Panoan group who speak a language relatively similar to theirs. In the same way that the Cashinahua do not like being called Cashinahua, those whom they call Yaminahua also use different names for themselves.

The older Cashinahua men told me that their group also used to wear decorations similar to those of the Yaminahua, First Shot, with an emphasis on body painting, tattoos, and the extensive use of colorful feathers. They also said they have always lived in contact with other groups, mentioning especially their friends the Iskunahua (Oriole people), other Panoan groups, and various Campa groups, who traveled through their areas. They often shared stories and songs, though they would never have permitted the other group's young men to move in and marry their young women.

Pudicho continues by including his group in his story.

> 8. At that time the Genuine people (Cashinahua) were living in the same region, and an outsider in a roofed boat arrived and began friendly relations with them. The Genuine men [sic] reciprocated, [individually] saying, "*Uiankavidi*, if you want me to work for you in this way, repeatedly bring me

---

[5]The Cashinahua attempt to indicate whether what they are saying is something witnessed or something told to them is much like the American English disclaimer, "I am told that..." The Cashinahua attach the reportative morpheme -*aki* to an independent clause which is normally at the end of a string of clauses that are grammatically chain-referenced to that independent clause. The independent clause also has a declarative mood affix -*ki* which means, 'I declare to you that...' The reportative morpheme -*aki* is the same affix -*ki*, with an action, indicating particle *a*- infixed in front of it. When combined -*kiaki* means 'I declare to you that he/she declared that...'

things." So the Genuine men collected rubber (caucho) and stockpiled it for the outsider boss. He came and took the rubber downriver and returned a month or so later, bringing them things. In exchange for the rubber, he was continually bringing them mosquito nets, blankets, cloth, pots, bowls, and beads. So they lived in this peaceful relationship trading with the outsiders.

9. On each of the rivers they peacefully contacted the outsiders long ago and collected rubber for them. In order to get nice things, they regularly made good things and traded them: new woven hammocks, handmade artifacts and feather headdresses, in addition to the caucho rubber. Getting good things, they continued to trade and live with the outsiders, so I was told.

However, from the very beginning the river traders had the advantage of knowing the value of the things they provided, relative to the amount of rubber they took downriver. One explanation for the peaceful nature of this contact is that they were not in the zone where the highly productive seringue rubber trees *(Hevea brasiliensis)* grow—the type that has to be scored each day to make the sap run. These indigenous people were probably living farther up river, where only the caucho rubber tree *(Castilloa elastica)* grows, which must be felled to extract its sap. Thus, they were not in direct competition with the Brazilian rubber tappers, who were ferociously anti-Indian (Hemming 1987:303–306).

During this peaceful era, when the Cashinahua were seeking the best situation in relation to the outsiders, Nacimiento, the oldest man I knew among the Cashinahua in Peru, was born in some isolated headwaters location. He tells what he was told as follows.

In order to create me, my father made my mother his wife when they were over on the other side [Embira]. While he was living on the other side, my father started to create me by sexually penetrating my mother. After he had loaded me into her and I was alive in my mother, my father came over in this direction [Curanja] to see and visit the outsiders. He abandoned her and I was a child without a father to provide for me after birth, so I was told.

Later while I was being born, my paternal aunt was thinking, "I doubt if the baby's father will come back from over there to live here again," so she began hitting me with a stick to kill me. Not having accepted me, she began hitting me with a stick. Then my paternal grandfather, my namesake, the one who namesaked me long ago, became angry at her and said, "You always eat my game! You always eat my garden produce! Don't ever again eat my garden produce! Don't ever again eat the meat that I shoot! Not wanting to namesake this child to me, are you hitting it to kill it?" After he spoke this, my paternal aunt went to where I lay and accepted me long ago, even though she had tried to club me to death, so I was told.

She picked me up and washed me—I don't remember any of this. After she had washed me, she said to my paternal grandfather, "Father! Today I have namesaked him to you. Don't be angry with us anymore, because I have namesaked him to you!"

Then he said to my mother and aunt, "Good! Always act this way towards me! This is the way I am. By namesaking this child after me today, you have made things all right!"

While we were settled in that place, I was growing; I was growing but I was not big yet. Then my collective male parent group, who had come over here to look around, left from this side [Curanja] and went back to Brazil, to where I was and then they took me to the Embira River—I don't remember this either. Then bringing me back in this direction, they settled on the upland between the small streams of the Embira headwaters. And my father raised me by hunting and planting gardens, so I was told.

Nacimiento was about five years older than Pudicho but was not a storyteller; he always said, "I am just a worker. I plant lots of cassava, corn, and peanuts; my people always eat well." However, with Pudicho's help, he told me about his early years.

The Cashinahua view early marriages as unstable, and a marriage is not considered permanent until a husband and wife have considerable investment in two or three children, of which they hope some are daughters. In Nacimiento's situation his father had gone off looking for a more advantageous situation and they were not certain he would return, so his mother and aunt tried to kill him. The grandfather who saved him may have been his father's father or a man who was of the same moiety, two generations up, and willing to enter into a special relationship with him by sharing a Genuine name. These Genuine names recognize a human body as a person and place that person, male or female, into a moiety and generational set; these generational sets alternate through time. And because he had a male sponsor, Nacimiento was kept alive until his father could take responsibility for him.[6]

Pudicho continues his story of peaceful relationships and begins to involve his immediate family.

> 10. While our ancient ones lived in this manner, the outsiders increased in all locations and established themselves on each of the large rivers. The Genuine men became accustomed to the outsiders' presence and worked for them, getting paid with cloth for their wives. After the outsiders had developed a friendly working relationship, they took the Genuine people downriver to work for them and lived with them for many years, so I was told.
>
> 11. After they made peaceful contact with the outsiders in all locations long ago, the ancient ones of my people—those who first started to exist long ago—engendered my father and my mother. Then later they engendered me, so that I would come into existence. My grandfather, who was very old and weak, saw me for a period of time long ago, so I was told.

Even though Pudicho's people were living in a remote southern corner of the Juruá River basin, like others, they traveled the uplands and received accounts of the increasing seasonal presence of the outsiders. In those early years the area that is now the Brazilian province of Acre and the headwaters of the Juruá and Purús rivers (now Peruvian territory) were claimed by Bolivia, which tried to govern the area and collect taxes. However, most of the men who came during the dry season to collect rubber were Peruvians and Brazilians. The former usually came up the Yavari River or over trails from the Ucayali Valley, and the latter came up the Juruá and Purús rivers. They spread out to work areas claimed by bosses, either tapping trees themselves or pressing Indians into working for them. The vast majority had no allegiance to Bolivia and resisted paying taxes (Hemming 1987:278, 305–306).

Pudicho also gave a quick background summary of his particular ancestral group. Each Cashinahua has a classificatory kinship relationship with every other Cashinahua, based on each one's Genuine name. However, they prefer to live with close relatives and to accept only sons of close

---

[6]The namesaking process does not necessarily have to include a living sponsor. The child may be given the name of a dead relative of the same moiety and same sex, two generations past. (For a more complete explanation see Kensinger 1995:138–139, 145.)

Initial Contact

relatives to move in and marry their daughters. Pudicho tells us that when various Cashinahua leaders and their followers were taken downriver they formed a new social grouping which resulted in his conception and birth. Pudicho continues with more details.

> 12. But before I was born, when my people had contacted the outsiders and were living among them in order to get things, my father and my mother grew up in the same communal house, and my father, who was older, made my mother, who was younger, his wife, so I was told. However, after they made him to have a wife and he took my mother, she rejected him for a while. But he finally won her over and engendered me, so I was told. While I was a child, they brought me to this river, to raise me in a peaceful isolated place without sickness and other problems. So on this other river I have lived peacefully.
>
> 13. But before all this happened, my father, my grandfather, and the ancient ones existed downstream on the With-Sun, so I was told; the river's name was "With-Sun". In order for the Genuine people to name that river, With-Sun, a Genuine man got lost long ago. After a Genuine man got lost and slept in the jungle, he traveled across level terrain without streams to follow and finally descended to a downstream section of the With-Sun. He had come to a large river; after sleeping on a level section of the uplands, he had descended to a large river and saw a straight stretch of river that did not have trees hanging over it and had lots of sunlight pouring in and reflecting off the water; it all looked good to him and he named it With-Sun, so I was told. My ancient one's name was Utudukun; he established that river's name long ago, so I was told.
>
> 14. When you are establishing a river's name, you should make yourself think, "What does it have?" Thus, you are able to give a name to a river.
>
> At that time, that Genuine man was thinking, "I descended to this river after I got lost yesterday. I came intending to shoot game, got lost on the uplands and today I came down to this river. The water is not hidden and the sun is coming in." As Utudukun sat there with the sun on his back, he thought, "Intending to name it, I can make myself to think, 'What does it have?' It is with Sun; nothing is hiding it and

the sunlight is coming in. I have made its name real today," he said and left.

15. Then a little while later his people were coming along continually crying out in order to find him and take him back home. As they came along crying out, they encountered Utudukun and asked, "Where were you last night?" He answered, "I arrived at a level place by a really large river and slept. After I slept, I went down to this real river thinking, 'What is it with?, so as to be able to name it.' I descended to it and I am now returning from naming it With-Sun. Then someone said, "You are returning from naming it With-Sun. Go and show it to me! Let me see that With-Sun, let's go!" So he took his people to see it and they established its name With-Sun long ago, and then lived on that river.

16. However, the outsiders were continually telling the Genuine people, "It is the Embira. This river is the Embira." By means of outsider words they named it the "Embira" long ago. The Ancient Ones used to call a different river "With-Red-Macaw" long ago, so I was told. While they were calling that river "With-Red-Macaw", the Ancient Ones were naming another river "With-Tub", so I was told. While the Ancient Ones were calling one river "With-Red-Macaw" and another river "With-Tub", the Genuine people were also calling it "With-Tub", so I was told. Even though they were saying, "This is the With-Tub," the outsiders called that large river "Juruá". When they were with the Genuine people, they told them, "It is the Juruá." The outsiders named it "Juruá" for them even though the Genuine people intended to call it "With-Tub".

17. Now a different river over on the other side [Juruá basin], another large river which they had possessed, the Brazilians were calling "Tarauacá". While the outsiders were calling it "Tarauacá", our Ancient Ones, my Ancient Ones, named it "Jungle-Turkey-Fell-In", so I was told. When my Ancient Ones called that river "Jungle-Turkey-Fell-In", the outsiders used to call another large river "Juruá".

18. The river which the outsiders called "Purús", we also always call it the "Purús" and live on it; I was told that my Ancient Ones used to call it "Large-River-Jungle-Turkey-Fell-In."

Initial Contact

> However, when the ancient ones were calling the other large river "Tarauacá" because of the outsiders, they continued to call its large tributaries by their own names: "With-Paucar", "With-Xana-Tree", "With-Yarina-Palm", "With-Hot-Peppers", and "With-Sun", they called them.
>
> 19. There on those rivers the Ancient Ones were engendering children; dwelling there on the edges of those rivers, they were engendering children to their wives. At the same time the elderly ones, those who first made contact with the outsiders, were growing weaker and dying off all over the region; however, their children were growing up. My father grew up with them and then engendered me.

Pudicho thus tells the extent of the area inhabited by those whom his core group considered their people. His son and two living brothers told me that there were lots and lots of them. The word translated Ancient Ones may be a little confusing; Pudicho uses it first in a general sense to mean all the Panoan groups who were like his father's group. But in text block 17 he narrows it to, "our Ancient Ones, my Ancient Ones" to indicate his father's immediate ancestral group. Thus, the river names were probably names used by the related Panoan dialects. All the rivers and streams named above are tributaries of the Juruá River, indicating that they lived mainly on that drainage before the disruption caused by the rubber boom.

The extent of the Cashinahua's habitation is confirmed by a Brazilian Army officer, Luiz Sombra, who was posted to that area. He disagrees, however, with the peacefulness of the contacts and wrote about the violent situations which probably contributed to the coming revolt by the Cashinahua (Sombra 1913). Portions of what he wrote in the Rio de Janeiro newspaper, *Jornal do Commercio,* follow.

> In February of 1905 I was in military service in the Upper Juruá under the orders of Dr. Colonel Sir Thaumaturgo de Axevedo, the hard-working and active administrator of the Department of Acre; he has since been promoted to General. At that time I was suddenly surprised with orders to become the General's representative in the Upper Tarauacá, a little-known region of that department, whose local administrative position was being assigned to me.
>
> According to the instructions attached to the edict of my appointment, I was invested with total power to control and suppress all persecution of Indians which was going on up

and down that river. This was not only happening in that area, but in the entire Amazon Basin where Indians were being persecuted and ill-treated by many rubber tappers during the rubber season.

I put all my energy to that task despite the risk to my life, the sacrifice of my health, and the growing animosity of some of the many well-to-do who dominated those faraway areas. The majority of the inhabitants had a ferocious prejudice against the Indians because they were heathens, or infidels, as the Peruvians point out. Thus, they did not prevent crimes against Indians nor their murder by professional killers, who are many times hired by Brazilians to push out or exterminate all the Indians living in the rubber tapping areas. The Indians are also freely exploited when they labor to extract rubber from the caucho tree.

During the unfolding of my difficult and dangerous task, I came to know some of the Indian tribes never before referred to in those regions of the Upper Amazon. Among the more than twenty tribes I know of by experience or have information concerning, the most remarkable are the Cachinauas, who distinguish themselves from the other tribes by their easy-going and laborious disposition, and by being the most numerous among the many tribes that still occupy the vast basin of the great Juruá River.

All the Indians of this tribe who were left on the Tarauacá lived in their communal houses *(malocas)* on the nonflooding lands up behind the rubber-tapping areas on the right-hand side from the delta of the Chiruan River up to the headwaters of the little river called the La Liberdade. And where they live elsewhere scattered in the communal houses of those who took refuge in the furthest floodplains of the upper Tarauacá, they are annually victimized by cruel raids. This leaves us with no information concerning those Cachinauas who were left hidden near some tributaries of the lower Juruá.

Presently, they are concentrated mostly on the previously referred to Liberdade, near where until 1906 they suffered great massacres on some tributaries of the Upper Tarauacá and the Upper Gregorio River, which has a tributary called the Flood Plain of the Cachinaua. They also have other principal communal houses on the dry upland between the Upper Envira River and the Upper Murú River, especially on the banks of the side stream called Iboassu, where I visited them in 1905 and 1906. (Sombra 1913:paragraphs 1–6)

Captain Sombra's information paints a much more hostile atmosphere where Indians were used, as he says, "for the pleasure of verifying the good aim of their rifles!" He was part of the first wave of Brazilian authority to enter the area after Brazil bought that territory from Bolivia. The fact that Brazil was active in taking control of the territory is reflected in Pudicho's next story segment.

> 20. While I was growing as a young child, a Peruvian outsider said to my father, "Work for me." By bringing him into a work relationship, he became the boss of my father's life long ago, so I was told. After that Peruvian boss made himself his owner, he made my father work while he lived with them, repeatedly leaving and returning. Then a different boss, a Brazilian, displaced the Peruvian and became the boss.

In many respects, the far headwaters of the Embira River were almost as close to the world market by mule trail back to the Ucayali River in Peru as by the 3,000 mile trip down the Juruá and the Amazon rivers to the Atlantic Ocean. Also, the tax collectors could be avoided by the former route. Peruvian rubber bosses were active in the Alto Juruá and Purús rivers, which is one of the reasons why Peru prevented Brazil from occupying those areas even though they thought they had bought them from Bolivia. The change in the status of the territory is signaled in Pudicho's narrative by the Peruvian being displaced by a Brazilian rubber boss; this provides a rough date of 1905 for this point in Pudicho's story.

As the outsiders were moving into their areas, the Cashinahua people and the other Ancient Ones were not at first concerned, because the outsiders who collected the seringue rubber only came in the dry season (Hemming 1987:296). And those who wanted the caucho rubber had to move on after all the trees in an area had been felled. The rubber was something that had no direct value in the indigenous cultures, and they liked the cloth and tools they got for their labor. Also, they already knew from their folklore that the Ancient Ones had lived near other people long ago, and by means of their own superior abilities had lived better in the forest than those other powerful outsiders. The story that Pudicho told me about that long ago time deals with Ancient Ones living near Inka, who did not know how to live in the rain forest. This Inka probably refers to mountain people who moved into the rain forest. The other Panoan language groups, who live in the Ucayali Valley, have many Inka stories that refer to people who live in the mountains. Pudicho told me the following.

> At the new first creation when Genuine people were coming into being, they were learning edibles. Being alive and learning, they were learning which plants to eat; they were learning which animals they could eat; they were learning to work. They were continually learning whatever there was to learn, so I was told.
>
> One of the Ancient Ones, Inka, was fat and not very knowledgeable; he had the quality of being unknowing. Kuman learned and thought up things for him long ago, so I was told. Kuman was a leader of the Ancient Ones and another leader, Inka, settled his people near Kuman's people. Then he said to Kuman, "What are we to do? What can we eat? There is nothing to eat! Let's plant produce crops." So they were creating manioc and corn; they were creating peanuts, bananas, *sacha papa, yubin,* sweet potatoes, and *ashipa;* they were creating and planting all the various crops long ago; Inka and Kuman created these plants together, so I was told.
>
> I was told that Inka did not know how to live in the jungle. After he had settled, he said, "Friend Kuman! Let's cut a garden and plant our crops!" After they had opened a new garden, they planted their crops: manioc, peanuts, *sacha papa, yubin,* and *yuxu.* The last thing they put in the ground was corn, when the sun came out and showed itself during the dry season. When the *yukan* tree was budding out to flower, they planted peanuts. However Inka, not being very knowledgeable, always planted his peanuts on the upland away from the streams; in the center of his garden this fat ignorant one always planted his peanuts. I was told that only Kuman knew how to do it correctly.
>
> When Inka wanted to make a garden for planting, he said, "Let's make gardens," and he chose a good spot. Then after they had cleared all the underbrush, they started sweeping away the dry leaves. They used sticks to push the fallen partially rotten limbs to the edge where they made piles. Starting from the uphill side they swept the ground bare using twigs with their leaves still attached. Next he said, "Let's fell the trees." Felling the trees all over the place, they littered the clean ground with branches. They cut the trees in

pieces, throwing away the small branches and the branches they could get their hands around, and piled the larger pieces without burning them. They left the ground unburned and planted their crops. As the crops were growing and the edible parts started maturing, they ate the soft corn, small manioc tubers, and the immature bananas. Later when the bananas were fat and mature, they made sweet banana drink and enjoyed it.

Then in order to make a new garden they said, "Again let's make another garden," and they started to do it as they had done at first. As Inka and Kuman were working, Kuman was thinking about the process. They swept away the leaves, felled the trees and were working very hard at cutting and throwing away the branches, when Kuman thought up the way we do it now. It was the beginning of the dry season and they were clearing two nearby hilltops when it began thundering. "Inkaa! The rains will be starting. Why are we doing it this way? Let's not sweep the dry leaves off," Kuman knew what to do and was thinking, "Inka doesn't know what to do." Kuman's people had finished cutting all the underbrush right up to the edge of the area that they wanted to clear on the hilltop. Then Kuman said, "Inkaa! Sweeping away the leaves and junk is difficult. After I fell the trees, I want to burn everything."

Inka replied, "You are wrong. Kuman, you will do poorly. You are going to kill your crops. If you burn and then plant, you will be doing bad."

But Kuman said, "It is not as you say. I will not do it wrong. I am doing good; I intend to do it." Then they finished felling the trees but did not cut them in pieces. They only cut the limbs that were sticking up in the air; they cut all the limbs and brush down to about two feet above the ground. They then let it all dry in the hot sun for a month or so and it finally lay there very dry. At that same time Inka was having his people sweep the leaves off to the side and had not yet had them fell the trees. Kuman said to himself, "I intend to burn my garden. I want to burn his also," and then burned his new garden long ago, so I was told.

Kuman was learning when he started the fire. The flames burned the dry stuff on the ground; the flames burned the dead trees at the edge of the forest. Many of the tree limbs were left as upright sticks of charcoal, but most of it burned completely. And then as it was cooling, Kuman was coming to see it when Inka said to him, "Kuman! Did you do wrong?"

Kuman replied, "Did I do wrong? Go look at what I burned. Let's go and look at it." So they went and looked; Inka said, "Wow, Kuman! You have done it very, very well. Friend, I am going to do the same." Because he had only cut the underbrush, he said, "I also will do the same. Let's continually do it the same way. In the same way you did well, let's only do it that way in the future and not sweep the leaves away." Then he also cut the trees and burned his new garden long ago, so I was told.

After he had done that he worked with Kuman and they were planting their crops, when Inka's people wanted to do the same thing, with each man saying, "May I do the same? Me too, may I also?" They cut the underbrush, felled the trees and prepared it for burning. All his people, working together, made long ridgetop gardens and burned them. "This is good. Let's only do it this way in the future, continually," they were saying as they collected side sprouts from banana plants and set them in rows across the long gardens to divide them into family sections. Then they divided up their family sections to plant manioc, *sacha papa, yubin,* sweet potatoes, *siu,* papaya, sugar cane, *shipa,* lima beans, cotton, and achiote. Then when the crops sprouted and leafed out, the fields darkened as the crops were growing. After that the corn, which they had poked into the ground, stood up with the other crops and was darkening the ground underneath. Then Inka said, "Wow, let's always do it only this way. Let's never again sweep the leaves aside without burning. This is the way to do it!" Thus, they learned to make gardens as Kuman thought it up long ago, so I was told.

After their gardens were well-established, Inka built a real house. He cut and set the upright support posts; put up the cross pieces and then ran double stringers the length of the house on top of the ends of the cross pieces, directly over the support posts. He lashed these all together with cotton cord, as was their custom long ago. Inka had ordered his wife, saying, "Wife, roll our cotton yarn together into cord for me." She took the homespun cotton yarn that they normally spun and twisted several strands of it into cord. After he had lashed on the cross pieces and lengthwise stringers, he set strong forked pieces on the centers of the crosspieces to support the long multipiece ridgepole which was also lashed on with the same cotton cord. He then cut long saplings for rafter poles and lashed them to the ridgepole, laying across the stringers, reaching almost to the ground. Next, he tied on the Yarina palm leaves which he had cut and dried. Using a long bone needle, he continually tied the leaves on both sides, meeting at the top, and then capped it off with a woven mat of palm leaves. It was in this type of house that they lived long ago.

Kuman also learned to build this type of house long ago, so I was told. As he was learning, he said to himself, "What a pity! What can I do? I don't have any cotton cord. With what can I tie it together? I can't do it, Inka. I will give it some thought!" Thinking, he thought of *nixpudun* and *xeu*, straight jungle vines. He collected them and used them to tie his house together long ago, so I was told.

However, as he was tying the cross pieces to the support posts, Inka asked, "Kuman, what are you doing?"

"I am not doing it as you did. Because I don't have cotton cord, I am doing it like this. Let's do it this way in the future," Kuman replied.

"You are doing it wrong! Yours will break apart. Vines are bad!" Inka said.

"Vines are not bad. It is yours that is bad; you do it with bad cord. I intend to do it this way," Kuman replied, and continued tying the house parts together. Then he said to himself, "I intend to do it like this. I need more vine," and went looking. He collected in coils *jexi* vine and new strong sprouts of *tene* vine, that went up a tree, and brought them back.

Then Inka said, "Kuman, are you going to tie your leaves on with this?"

Kuman said, "By means of these, I am going to do it; with these I will tie on the leaves." Then with just vines he started; by splitting the larger vines in half he was continuously tying on the palm leaves.

Inka again said, "You are doing it wrong! You are causing it to leak and drip. When yours leaks, you will come and sit below my hammock. You are making your house in a bad manner."

Kuman again replied, "I am not doing it wrong. I am doing it this way." He tied the leaves on one side of each section by continuously tying with one long vine up each rafter pole until the leaves reached the top of that side. And then he put leaves on the other side the same way, until they reached the peak. Then he went and got *xenpan* palm leaves and wove them together as a cap for the peak of the house and put it on. Then he got more *yarina* palm leaves and made a second covering to put over the first ridge cap. After the first cap was in place, he pushed sticks horizontally through both caps and tied each securely by passing the tie vines under the ridgepole, pulling the ends of each stick down snugly, and said, "In this manner I did it today! Kuman did it!"

Inka had not finished his roof yet; because he was fat, he was behind in tying on his leaves. Then there came the roar of rain marching through the forest and lots of rain began to fall. Kuman had already moved into his house to sleep and stay out of the sun. As he was there during the rain, there were no leaks and it stayed dry all night long. In the morning the water was still pouring off just the lower edge of the leaves, and Kuman said out loud to himself, "Ah, you made it very good!"

Inka came and said, "Kuman! You have done well. Let's do it this same way continually from now on. And as you have done it, I also intend to do it. I also intend to do it the same way." He went and got vines; he also got *nixpudun* and *xeu* vines and began to think, "It was like this that Kuman did it," as he tied the cross pieces and all the other parts of the frame together. Then he got *yarina* palm leaves and as he was thinking, "Kuman did it this way," he also used *tene* and *jexi* vines to tie all his leaves on the rafter poles. And then said, "Kuman, let's continually make houses this way. We shall do it this way." It was like this when Kuman thought up how to make a correct house long ago, so I was told.

The story goes on for almost four more notebooks. Inka and Kuman go hunting and build temporary shelters; Inka's leaks and Kuman does it correctly. They cook corn; Inka waits for water to boil and Kuman roasts his in the coals and eats first. They go hunting and are too slow to grab animals, so Kuman innovates and makes the first bow and arrow. From then on Kuman is the fountain of all knowledge, even discerning which plants are useful to cure various snake bites. This is the tradition that assured the Ancient Ones that they could deal with the rubber collectors, the newer outsiders. But Pudicho's group loses patience with the outsiders, as he relates in the next chapter.

3

The Escape

Normally, each Cashinahua communal house functioned separately with its own headman, but the rubber bosses liked to work with one person, holding him responsible for the actions of the others. The Cashinahua continue to have one headman per village, and leadership is conferred on the basis of ability and character. The following revolt took place on the Embira River after the move downriver told by Pudicho in text block 10.

> 21. At first this Brazilian boss made friends with the Genuine headman, Chanemaiti, who, even though he lived in a different communal house, acted as leader of all the men from the other houses, coordinating the collection of rubber, the making of gardens, and the raising of crops. When there was enough rubber, Chanemaiti went downriver with the Brazilian boss by motorboat and brought back things for his people. By saying, "We intend to get things for you," and by taking Chanemaiti downriver, the Brazilians were making them and others, who lived downstream, their property. After initially befriending and making them their own, the Brazilians began drinking rum, the biting liquid that someone magically changed long ago, verbally abusing the Genuine men [sic], who had settled there, and sexually using their wives to their detriment.

This early economic arrangement was different from the later debt peonage system in which each person was given things on credit and then tried to work off the debt. At that time, even though they were living in several separate communal long houses, the entire group of Cashinahua was working together. Their paramount leader, Chanemaiti, acted as coordinator and guarantor and was responsible for dividing the goods among the men after he had gone downriver with the rubber boss. This was a good arrangement for the Brazilian boss because he was getting rubber for a meager investment. Friendship and the promise of trade goods works well in the wilds of Amazonia, even today, if fulfilled. The rubber boss acted uprightly at first, but the rum produced in Brazil brought out his true attitude towards women. Since only a few rubber collectors brought their wives from their home areas, many Brazilians found that a gift of cloth could tempt most young women.

Among the Cashinahua the husband/wife relationship was a relatively open one. The Cashinahua women have a long tradition of having lovers in addition to their husbands. This is especially prevalent during the early marriage period, and it often involves gifts from the lover. They also believe that it takes sustained sexual intercourse to produce a child. Casual sex in exchange for cloth would appeal to the women because they may have thought that the men were getting more trade goods than they were. The anthropologist Janet Siskind (1973), who worked with the Sharanahua in Peru during the 1960s, relates that some women still exchanged sex for trade goods at that time. The Cashinahua were living upriver on the Curanja at the time of Siskind's report, and the same river traders who worked with the Sharanahua worked also with the Cashinahua and continued to do so into the 1970s when we were there. I did not hear any stories of Cashinahua women trading sex for trade goods, but there were many things I was not told about.

> 22. Finally the men rebelled, saying, "Why do these outsiders live badly among us, making us work hard and mistreating us by sexually using our wives? Let's get out of here and go live without problems! We can live in peace if we move to the isolated upland areas. The outsiders are bad, let's kill them. Let's kill all the outsiders and keep on killing them in the future! Otherwise, they will take away all the women and we will be without wives." Saying this all around, the Genuine headman of each house agreed to kill the outsiders, so I was told.

The Cashinahua were never pacifists; they killed game animals as well as enemies with an equally dispassionate sense of need and duty. The women may have had the freedom to accept bribes from the boss and his helpers occasionally, but the men were more worried about the women

The Escape

leaving them and moving in with outsiders. They had heard that other women were doing this on other rivers so they reacted.[7]

> 23. With Chanemaiti leading the men, they shot the outsider boss first and then killed all of his helpers, including their wives and children. Then in order to get his things, Chanemaiti split open the chest where he stored the rifle cartridges and divided them among all those who had carbines, and then they entered his storehouse to divide all his things among themselves. They took large quantities of knives, machetes, and axes. They also took large quantities of clothing, cloth, iron pots, bowls, plates, and all types of cups; they completely took all his things in revenge. The other outsiders were permanently settled downriver, but this one Brazilian boss had settled my people near his own house, which was isolated from the other outsiders. After they shot the outsider boss, my people escaped over to this side [Curanja] long ago to produce children for a period of time, so I was told.

Pudicho indicates that they had lived in peace with the outsiders up to that time. This was remarkable, considering that they must have known about and been affected by the violence that had developed on the other rivers. The clashes between the indigenous groups and the rubber tappers were documented by Constant Tastevin, a Roman Catholic missionary who served on the middle Amazon River and in the Juruá basin from 1906 to 1926 and took time to visit and inquire. He knew the name Kachinaua [Brazilian spelling], but used the name *Huni-Kuin*, which was used by most of the Panoan-speaking groups in the Alto Juruá area to identify themselves. Tastevin wrote:

> Before the arrival of the *seringueiros* from northeastern Brazil, the Murú was inhabited only by savage Indians. They were more concentrated in this region than anywhere else. Most of them spoke the Pano dialect and called themselves *Huni-Kuin*, 'the real men'. They were divided into many

---

[7]The priest Constant Tastevin wrote prior to 1920, "All these tribes [in the Tarauacá and Upper Juruá drainage] have already found themselves in contact with civilized tribes...soon they will be nothing more than a memory, for their women like very much to marry whites and mulattos..." (Tastevin 1943:3, 24, 63). Since Pudicho's people were spread out on almost all the rivers, I think it logical that some of their women may have moved in with rubber tappers because they wanted things. John Hemming stated: "With such an acute shortage of women, Indian tribes were harassed for their girls as much as for the labour of their men" (Hemming 1978:297).

groups, sometimes allied, sometimes hostile. The most important tribe was that of the Kachinaua (vampire men) who settled particularly along the right affluents of the middle Murú. At first they accepted the presence of *seringueiros* without hostility, but gradually, jealousy, the extreme differences in mentality, language, culture, religion, and customs of the two races caused conflicts that from an initial skirmishing ended in merciless warfare. First the *caucheros,* that is the Peruvians who were the pioneer exploiters of *Castilloa elastica,* which must be felled before being used, and then the *seringueiros,* or Brazilians, armed raiding expeditions to dislodge the Indians from their homes and let the civilized people work in peace. Today [before 1925] there is but a single organized tribe [community] of Kachinaua. It is established at Bôa Vista, on the right bank of the Humaytá, and includes no more than twelve families with only 31 members: 12 men, 13 women, 2 girls, and 4 boys. This demonstrates that infant mortality and birth control contribute as much to the extermination of the Indians as their destruction by man. Despite the abundant resources furnished by the state, the Positivist formula has shown its complete inadequacy. The Bôa Vista tribe lives on friendly terms with the *seringueiros* but visits them as little as possible. The chief once said to a young man who was afraid of being cheated by me: "Don't be frightened. This man is not a white like the others. He is a spirit sent by Kana. He won't cheat you." When a *seringueiro* appeared, all the women hastened to hide the smoked fish they had brought back the day before from the Tauaya.

The other Kachinaua families are scattered along the borders of the Murú and live more or less among the civilized people. There are two families above Bélem, four above Itaparica, seven at Paraiso, three at Guajara, eight at Aryopolis and about a half dozen on the Iboyassú. To complete the list we must mention the ten or so women who live with the *seringueiros.* (Tastevin 1943:62–63) [See Tastevin's map in appendix.]

Later Tastevin gave the following account of the rubber tappers.

The Murú has become the undisputed domain of the *seringueiros* who have conquered it by toil and strength of arms. Through their efforts, they have transformed the virgin forest which was merely a vast hunting ground for the Indians, into a rubber producing industry. The Indians compelled the *seringueiros* to use force by their repeated thefts and assassinations, generally committed with cowardice, ferocity, treachery, and revolting abuse of confidence. No one loves the Indians more than I. I visit them everywhere, instruct them, console them, encourage and advise them. I defend them to the limit of my poor means. I invoke the compassion and indulgence of Christians. I have combated consistently the prejudice which refuses to recognize the Indians as human beings because, as they have not been baptized, they have no souls. I explain that they are our equals, like the Jews and Musulmans [sic] who also are unbaptized. I try to assimilate them with the Brazilians because their only chance of salvation resides in the Positivist standpoint, unless, as in North America, the government decides to isolate them on reservations.

But unfortunately the Indians are proud and suspicious, and in their complacent ignorance, have only hatred and contempt for the civilized man. That does not prevent them from begging and being envious and insatiable, goaded by poverty. The *seringueiros* are good and generous, but they are poor, and the Indians do not understand the value of what they demand. This causes their dissatisfaction, which results in thefts, murders and reprisals.

The Christians first invaded the Murú River around 1890, and the massacres began in 1898. Nothing seemed simpler than to dispose of a troublesome tribe. Thirty to fifty men were armed with repeating rifles and approximately one hundred bullets each and during the night they surrounded the single communal dwelling, shaped like a beehive, where the Indians were sleeping peacefully. When the Indians arose at dawn to take their first meal and prepare for the hunt, a prearranged signal was given, and the attackers fired. Very few Indians escaped. The women and children, who could be taken, were led away into captivity, but no quarter was given to the men, who showed themselves indomitable and fearless. Happily this is ancient history now.

In general it was the half-civilized Peruvian rubber hunters who were most ardent in the massacre. To them the Indian was an irrational creature who could be killed like a monkey.

> But this was evidently an assertion they did not believe, for these men never ate Indian flesh.
>
> The Peruvian *caucheiros* disappeared about twenty years ago, after a brief appearance. Thanks to the rubber slump, the Brazilians themselves are on the decrease. Having lost all hope of making a fortune, those who were able to do so returned to their homes. The last official census in 1920 gave the Murú a population of 4,000, but the one I have just taken, as accurately as possible, credits the district with only half that number. (Tastevin 1943:66)

It is hard to say when what Tastevin relates took place. He was writing before his publication date of 1925 and was relating mostly oral history from an era that existed before he started working there in 1906, soon after Brazil took charge of the territory in 1903. So it is possible things were more peaceful on the Embira River for a longer time. Even if this were true, stories would have filtered over from the other rivers and made the Cashinahua men cautious and ready to strike first.

When Pudicho first told me the story of escape from Brazil, I tried to estimate the date of its occurrence. The Cashinahua are very careful in reckoning who is older and who is younger among them. Nacimiento said that Pudicho was about the size of a five- or six-year-old child at the time of the escape, and that he was the size of a ten-year-old. Grompes, Pudicho's son, says he took Maria as a wife just before a visit by the man from San Paulo (Schultz 1951) and when he was just old enough to have a wife, so he was born sometime around 1935. Pudicho says he was a grown man, not an adolescent, when Grompes was born, and had had other children earlier who all died. And Pudicho said that he was told that he was alive when the Peruvian was his group's boss, thus before 1904. So I estimate that the earliest date for the rebellion was 1908, and the latest was 1920, depending on how long the Peruvian boss stayed with his father's group after Brazil purchased the territory. Cecilia McCallum has a similar conclusion for a revolt between 1910 and 1920, based on her work with the Cashinahua who live downriver in Brazil on the Purús River (McCallum 1989:58). However, it may have been a different revolt.

Nacimiento's group did not go downriver and live with the same boss as Pudicho's father's group, but he indicates that there may have been more trouble than Pudicho put in his story. Nacimiento adds the following to his previous account.

> Then because we heard that outsiders had shot some of our people, they made me escape with them. I was about the size of a very young teenager and still growing when they

> brought me over in this direction. After I came to this river, I thought only of hunting and survived by eating what I hunted. Then my paternal grandfather came, the one who had namesaked me when they raised me without a mother [who had left]. As my thinking improved, he kept saying to me, "When you think, think of work! Think of hunting!"

This indicates that there was a general exodus of people directly related to Pudicho's group.

The name Cashinahua, whose spelling (Kachinaua, Kaxinawa, Cachinaua) varies with country and era (but all pronounced "Ka-she-na-wa") seems to have been a creation of the rubber tappers. Because they had learned some words in the indigenous dialects, they combined *kashi* 'bat' with *nawa* which they thought meant 'people'. They then probably used the name *kashinawa* to refer to a whole range of groups whose languages were all closely-related Panoan dialects.

The linguist Tastevin used the name *Kachinaua* in a generic sense and did not place it in a list of names that were given to him of people of the Tarauacá area. Some of these names are definitely from outside the designated group. Some were insulting and others ludicrous, e.g., *Mainaua* (earth people who live in holes like the armadillos) and *Tyuchunaua* (extinct flame people who live without fire). But he refers to all the groups as *Huni-kuin* 'Real people' (Tastevin 1943:62–64).

To this day, there is a difference between what people are called by outsiders or by other indigenous groups and what they call themselves. Pudicho's group maintains they never used any other name than *Huni Kuin* 'Real or Genuine people', but they are called *Sainaua* (hollering ones) by the Sharanahua-Marinahua-Mastanahua linguistic group, who now live on the main channel of the Purús River. Interestingly, "Sainaua" was a name reported to Tastevin for a group who had lived far up the Murú River and as of 1925 had crossed the Embira River (Tastevin 1943:63). This date would not have been much after the possible dates for Pudicho's group's escape.

The word *Cashinawa* 'vampire bat people' was never accepted by Pudicho's ancestors. To them it was and still is an insult. They say it was applied to all the groups that cooked and ate their own prominent dead as a reverential act. The Cashinahua in Peru told me that the eating of their dead was repulsive to the outsiders. Sombra (1913) wrote the following concerning this in his newspaper article.

> About their festivals, which I referred to earlier, the most curious concerns the funeral, of some *tucháua* [leader] or any personality of the *maloca* [communal housed], which lasts

three days; I only remember what happens on the first and second days. On the first, as on the last one, they speak honorably of the high virtues of the dead person. The corpse is eaten by his friends and relatives after being well roasted on a fire where the corpse is put with its head covered with a large clay pot in order to prevent any repugnant feelings among the dead one's tribesmen due to the contortions of the dead man's face during the roasting of the fire. When the corpse is a female the pubic area is also covered with some mud or pottery.

They all gather around the fire and sit there filling the air with loud screams until the corpse is roasted. Then they start to take pieces of the deceased to devour him while all present give off loud cries feeling sorry about the death of their chief or relative. The sadness they feel does not prevent the display of satisfaction on their faces as they taste so delicious a delicacy!

Each takes a chunk of meat by one's rank, according to closer or more distant relationship to the deceased, the closest relatives have precedence, starting with the widow, who was given preference on certain body parts considered the most flavorful. After the corpse's meat is eaten, the remains and bones are thoroughly toasted, then pulverized and mixed in a wooden container with *calçuma,* a beverage already described [crushed corn, peanuts, manioc boiled together], which is drunk by those honoring the funeral on its second day with the same cries and lamentations.

At the sight of this description, the reader should not feel that the Cachinauás are cannibals. They only eat the corpse of their chiefs and important relatives as a duty and also as a religious act; they neither kill for eating nor devour their enemies whom they kill, on the contrary, in respect to them they bury the enemy chiefs who fall in combat. (Sombra 1913:paragraphs 78–81)

Returning to the escape, Pudicho says:

24. From there all the Genuine headmen, they were grown men, the grandchildren of the Ancient Ones, were escaping with their people. On their trip coming in this direction, they came upriver and then followed a stream until it disappeared. Then they came across the high jungle where there are no streams until they had entered another stream

drainage. Then after they crossed a small stream that would have water in it all year, they settled there and made gardens long ago, so I was told.

They escaped up the Embira River; whether they used the Brazilians' canoes and boats is not known. They always said that they did not learn to make and use dugout canoes until they made contact on this side [Curanja]. Araguana, Pudicho's sister's husband, tells about this later in his part of this story. Even if they had a few canoes, most of the travel would have been on foot because they soon followed streams too small for canoes.

The purpose phrase, "to produce children," at the end of text block 23, is important because it expresses something very important about their way of life. In their make-use-discard society at that time, nothing was considered permanent except perhaps their stone axes. Land was cleared, used, and abandoned. Houses were built, lived in, and then left behind after four or five years. Weapons, tools, pots, hammocks, and utensils were replaced regularly. Even the manufactured goods taken from the Brazilians were soon gone. The only thing of lasting value which was worth investing in were human relationships. The most important of these were the parent-child relationship, especially with daughters. So they needed to settle down to produce children.

Pudicho's group had a difficult time finding an isolated place to settle because they had crossed into Peruvian territory. At that time there was a major mule trail leading from the Embira River up to a major trail junction at a place called Varadero and then on down the Inuya River to the Ucayali River (see Tastevin's map in the appendix). And even though world rubber prices had begun to fall in 1913, the Peruvians were still searching up and down each stream for any caucho trees that had escaped them. This led to a confrontation which Pudicho relates.

> 25. After they made gardens and were living there, some outsiders again contacted them long ago, so I was told. When some Peruvians made contact with them, the Genuine men said among themselves, "Months ago we were able to shoot Peruvians. Let's kill them." Then the Peruvian boss asked them, "Did you shoot a boss and come in this direction some months ago?"
>
> One of the Genuine headmen said, "I did not shoot anyone. We were only collecting rubber some months ago." Having tricked the outsider boss, he grabbed him and shot him. But the Peruvian boss returned the fire and they killed each other. As the two lay there, the Genuine men shot and killed

all of the other outsiders. Then they left that area and traveled in this direction in a wild area very far from here. They descended onto this Curanja River, so I was told; by means of it I have lived.

26. After my people descended to the headwaters of this Curanja River, they did not have any place else to go; not having any place to go, they settled there and made gardens, so I was told. When they had cut new garden plots, the children of the ancient ones, grown men and grown women, settled there and were producing children. After they cut and burned the new garden plots, the men returned repeatedly to their old gardens and brought back very small garden plants. They planted cassava, bananas, *sacha papas,* corn, peanuts, *sacha camote,* sweet potatoes, papaya, sugar cane, and a different kind of cane for making arrows. After they did that and could eat the produce of the new gardens they continually replanted them so that they were producing bountifully. Then they cut other garden plots, left them to dry thoroughly, and burned them off to plant new crops. Then, so that they could stay together, they built a long communal house on a high flat area near their gardens.

The flat-topped hills of the Curanja valley are the remnants of an ancient sea bottom that has been eroded by rivers and streams (Meggers 1971:8). These well-drained hills are still preferred for gardens. The Cashinahua located their houses here before they again became dependent on contact with the outside world and moved down to live by navigable waters. Pudicho has used his last reportive "...so I was told" in text block 25, thus signaling that he is henceforth referring to his own experiences and memories.

Nacimiento told me that he came to know Pudicho at the time they built their long houses on the upper Curanja River and helped teach him to hunt. In 1974, the Cashinahua village of Balta on the Curanja had a sudden influx of about 150 Cashinahua visitors from the Tarauacá River area of Brazil. Many of the older men in that group told me that they were born in that far headwaters area and knew Nacimiento and Pudicho as young men before moving to Brazil. This area is still very wild and isolated and is now sporadically inhabited by a nomadic hunter-gatherer group, as related in the final chapter of this book.

4

Return to the Old Ways

Pudicho continues by telling what life was like as he remembered his early years while learning to be a member of his group.

27. While they were living there the things they brought with them long ago, after they killed the outsiders, began to be consumed and wear out: while hunting, the cartridges were being used up; while working, their clothes were wearing out, and they had no source for obtaining new ones. As they continued cutting down trees, their axes were worn down to almost nothing from frequent sharpening; and they kept breaking their machetes and knives; and they kept losing their fishhooks when the fish escaped with the hooks.

28. With all their things almost gone, my people were suffering privation and although they kept moving from place to place, they were not doing very well; their sharpenable tools, knives, machetes, and axes were wearing out. While their cartridges were being used up, their guns—lever-action carbines—were also going bad. My people had not seen shotguns; they had not been made yet. The outsiders had brought only lever-action carbines long ago.

29. So when the carbines were wearing out and the cartridges were being used up, they again learned to make arrows from wild cane. They collected the fruiting stalks of river cane when it was flowering, fitted arrow points to them and used them to shoot game; they were shooting tapir, deer,

spider monkeys, turkey-like *paujiles,* and howler monkeys. They lived by hunting and eating the meat. During this time they discovered genuine cane, cream-colored cane and orange-colored cane, which the ancient ones of some stone-axe people had planted. They dug these up and moved them to their own gardens so they could make arrows from the fruiting stalks.

During that time period Araguana, who was a little younger than Pudicho and later became Pudicho's sister's husband, learned to hunt using only their traditional methods. He tells it as follows.

How I started to grow long ago I intend to tell you; Listen!

My father raised me and my mother raised me; by means of her milk she made me grow. While feeding on her milk I stood up. After I had learned to stand and walk, I started to learn the difficulties of the bow and arrow. I started by using a child's arrow which my father made from the center spine of a palm frond. I pinched it on the bowstring to start shooting. Pinching it in front of the bowstring, without giving it a thought, I shot the child's arrow into the air for practice. I did not know anything yet because I had not shot anything. After I had grown a little more I shot a cricket with the child's arrow that my father had made for me. Not knowing how to really hunt, I continued for the time being shooting crickets and lizards; however, after growing some more I learned properly. I started learning by shooting doves from inside a palm leaf blind. The first time I shot a dove from inside a blind I took its head right off and it flopped all over the ground. I jumped out, grabbed it and said to my father, who was in a nearby blind, "Father, I shot a dove!"

However, he said, "Don't tell me! Go back in your blind for now." I went back in and all I did was sit and look at the dove; I had started real hunting by killing it. Then my father said, "Let's go," and took me back to our village. After we entered the house he said, "Don't eat it. It is said that it is bad luck to eat one's first kill. So don't eat it." So I abstained from eating any doves that I killed for the next several months, as my father had taught me. Then I started shooting rodents (*añuje*) from blinds which my father built for me in our manioc garden. Then I started to shoot deer using long arrows with broad bamboo points that my father made for me. Next I learned to shoot banded peccary. And then when I was a full-grown teenager [14 more or less] I shot my first tapir.

> Again saying, "Don't eat it!" they made me abstain from eating it. By doing all that they were making me do, I became a strong young man who was learning all that I needed to know.

Pudicho continues by telling how the grown men, who had become accustomed to using outsider guns, suffered having to return to bows and arrows.

> 30. Because the guns which they had gotten from the outsiders had worn out, my people were suffering privation and had to hunt with bows and arrows. The ones who were good shots and didn't usually miss got spider monkeys, howler monkeys, capuchin monkeys, *paujiles,* tapir, peccary, and deer. The less capable hunters shot some large game, a few deer, a few peccary, but not tapir or spider monkeys; their families were always in a pitiable state. But the really bad hunters could shoot only a few grouse-like birds with their arrows; eating these they lived in a state of privation.

Pudicho's son, Grompes, told me that back in those days, when they were living away from any outsider diseases, their population was much larger than it is now. The proportion of very young children, however, was much smaller because about one-half or more of the babies died in their first year, due to intestinal parasites and infections caused by unsanitary conditions. He said that the Ancient Ones lived in dirty conditions with dirt floors and did not know of the need to wash as they do now. As Araguana indicated, babies nurse until after they stand up and are not given much solid food until they have teeth; thus they are dependent on their mother's protein intake. The Cashinahua say they have always eaten lots of meat; not only do they like the taste of meat, they also believe that those who eat a lot of meat live better. Because most of their vegetable foods are bland tasting, they mix bits of meat with each bite of cassava root or boiled banana. Often the men do not want to eat unless they have at least a small amount of meat.

Pudicho continues by telling of more frustrations.

> 31. After they produced children, the men felt deprived, because they had no sharpenable tools and could not make new arrows. Then they came upon an old house site, where outsiders had started to live long ago, and found some tin cans; they cut these into pieces and fashioned them into knives. As they were fashioning the knives, they started to clear the undergrowth for a new garden, but the tin can metal edges

simply rolled over without accomplishing much. Living in this state of privation, we continually moved from place to place a long way from here.

Pudicho further includes himself by using "we" for the first time. The finding of an abandoned house site is a testimony to the penetration of outsiders into this remote area in search of rubber and is a clue to the time period. The world price of rubber began to fall in 1913 when East Indian rubber became available in quantity. This removed the profit margin from this remote area and provided the Genuine people a place to hide, again some time after 1920. The older men still had their stone axes and knew how to make machete-like undergrowth slashers from black palm wood. But because they had become accustomed to metal tools, they could or would not be satisfied with the traditional tools again. Grompes told me that Pudicho threw away the stone axe that his father had given him as he was dying. Yet, whenever the game animals became scarce they continually moved to secure meat, their most desirable food.

> 32. Those who originally contacted and shot the outsiders and then came over to this side [Curanja] were men with knowledge of strong potions. They used that medicine against some of our own people to kill them; the victims became sick and died; bad pains would enter them and they would die. Even women died; older women and younger women, who were approaching menopause, were dying. For many different reasons, the adults were dying off in all the communal houses; they were continually expiring in all locations.

The Cashinahua, both men and women, have an extensive knowledge of leaf medicines and use them even now—to calm babies, ease headaches, and treat various ailments. The word for 'medicine', however, can also mean 'black magic', a practice engaged in by men called *muka dauya* 'with bitter medicine'. This was done by the use of spirits, herbs, animal parts, or the victim's excrement. At first, I was told that all of these men and their apprentices had died in the various flu epidemics. Later, one of my neighbors told me that he had been an apprentice and that another man in Balta had been a 'man with bitter medicine' though he had ceased practicing what little he knew. And even though I asked pointedly, he would not identify the man. Even so, all of the adults are still careful to hide their excrement, and the fear of black magic was strong enough to cause the government-sponsored program to promote the use of pit privies to fail completely.

Pudicho continues by telling how people his age were trained.

> 33. During this time, as the children were growing up, their parents taught them to work. They taught the boys to work in the gardens. They taught them to shoot game, saying, "This is how it is done." They taught them to build houses, saying, "Build a house and you will have a place to hang your hammock." The women of the group taught the girls, who were with them, to spin cotton and weave hammocks, saying, "After you have spun cotton and made a hammock, you will sleep in it. In the future, make a hammock for your husband."

Belisario, Pudicho's youngest brother, tells of being raised in that isolation.

> After my father became afraid of the outsiders and escaped long ago, he engendered me up in the uplands; at the headwaters of the stream Tamaya in the village of Panavaiu-xun I was engendered and born. After I was born I knew to feel for my mother's breasts and nurse. And thus I began to grow. Later when I was crawling and starting to stand up my father was happy with me. While I was growing we lived on each of the uplands at the headwaters of the streams; it was there that I grew to maturity.
>
> However, back when I started growing my father made me a small bow and some palm frond spine arrows. I shot a cricket and started to become accustomed to the way I would shoot game animals when I grew up. Not only did I shoot crickets, I shot green lizards and black lizards. I shot minnows and small fish as I grew and changed each year. And while I was shooting small birds up in a tree, birds with beautiful feathers, my father saw that I had grown and made me a real bow and some real arrows. Then I shot small game like quail, *punchana*, and rodents as the years went by and when I was almost grown I began to think of learning to make gardens. After my father had cut a plot for a new garden, he taught me, saying, "After the garden site is cleared and burned, one can plant something." Then I helped him plant *sacha papa*, manioc, *sacha camote* and peanuts; I planted all types of garden plants.
>
> When it came to learning to build a house, it was like someone was telling me how to make all the house parts.

When my parents were teaching me to make the parts, I was listening and working as they were saying, "One can do it like this. When making things, one can do it this way." Thus, while I was living with them and growing I was learning everything, all their different types of work.

Pudicho continues by telling how children are named and included in their extended kinship system.

34. Several years after their parents died, they produced children in the same locations; they lived on in the same places to engender children. When the babies lived, the men namesaked the males to their aged fathers. When the women, who dwelt with them, got [conceived] female children, they namesaked them to their aged mothers. They continually named their children in all locations as they lived suffering the lack of sharpenable tools.

Bearing children is always important to the Cashinahua because their children are their old-age insurance. The children they raise to adulthood are acculturated to support the mother who raised them and a father if he stays with the mother.

Pudicho tells how the namesaking system normally operates as it places the children into the kinship system. The children are given a Genuine name of a paternal grandfather or a maternal grandmother who is theoretically of the same moiety as the putative father who establishes the moiety of the child. These are not Hispanic names. Being a closely-related namesake brings with it a sponsorship status which is advantageous to the child if the grandparent is young enough, as the story of Nacimiento's birth in chapter 2 illustrates. Actual grandmothers could be as young as 26 years older than the grandchild and actual grandfathers only 30 years older. The namesaked grandparent, however, could even be dead or of a classificatory relationship. The main function of the naming system is to place a person in a moiety and a marriage section which alternates generationally.

Pudicho continues by telling how the women faced up to their situation.

35. Everybody was suffering self pity when the outsider things were wearing out, the things that they brought after they shot the outsiders during the first contact: the sharpenable tools, axes, machetes, knives, the cloth, blankets, pots, bowls, little bowls, plates, little plates, and various types of cups. Then a woman came to a realization, saying, "Now that the things we got from the outsiders are about

gone, let's make clay pottery like we heard that our Ancient Ones did long ago." She tried to make a pot out of good red clay from the center of a stream and she tried to make a pot by using white clay, but they both cracked when they were fired. So, she tried again, getting clay from a different stream bank. She formed and dried the clay things well and they did not crack when fired; wanting to be good and sound, the clay things endured firing.

36. Then a lot of women thought that they could do the same and also collected clay. They made pots, large bowls, small bowls for drinking gruel, and jugs to get water for cooking and for drinking. They made larger pots and used them to cook gruel and large quantities of food. They filled these large pots to the brim with meat, peccary and deer, which the men had brought in and with cassava root, which they had gone and gotten from the gardens, and were boiling them together. While eating this, they said, "They knew how to eat and get by long ago. Doing as they did, we can do the same." Thinking this, they continually made pots, but unfortunately the pots eventually cracked and broke. And after they made other pots and used them for a while, these also cracked and broke; they lived continually making clay things back then.

The woman who made the first pots knew that her mothers and grandmothers had made pottery when they lived on the Embira River. She may have even seen her grandmother collect clay, coil the hand-made dowels of clay into the desired shape, and smooth it with a river-worn pebble. Her mother, however, had not taught her how because they had iron pots. This was a situation of knowledge without experience. But the knowledge was better than nothing, and so they were able to relearn old techniques. They celebrated their successes, but they were only rationalizing their pitiable situation. They still missed the trade goods that they had become accustomed to using.

37. Some of the Ancient Ones, those who were less ancient, were still alive at that time. The children, whom they had engendered, cared for them; their sons made gardens for them and were feeding them from them; their daughters cooked for them and fed them. Although they were becoming old women and old men and dying off in all locations, some of the less ancient ones remained and lived with their children.

However, everyone was suffering greatly because they had no place to get sharpenable tools and other things.

That some of their older people survived their time among the rubber collectors shows that the time with the outsiders was not extensive enough to disrupt family relationships and responsibilities. Because children and grandchildren are their only old-age insurance, household groups always consisted of three or four generations. The daughters stayed with their mothers, and the sons moved out to live in their wives' households. The daughters of the family took direct care of their parents and maternal grandparents. The brothers helped with labor and a portion of their hunt. But they feared the spirit of their relatives when they died. Babies, children, and adults who didn't have the power of knowledge were buried in the floor of the communal houses after all their possessions were completely destroyed. But adults, both men and women, "with knowledge" (any kind of knowledge that could be considered special) were cooked and eaten, as Pudicho describes.

> How they did long ago when a man died and they ate him, I intend to tell you. Listen!
>
> When one of the Genuine men was sick and died, they did not want a Genuine man's flesh to rot. So they said, "Let's eat him." While everybody was gathered all around wailing, they began tying him up with a rope, thinking, "His people must eat him."
>
> While they were trussing him up, the dead man's wife, who had not eaten for days, danced back and forth facing the body moving her hands, palms up, in a beckoning manner. While she did this, she was speaking to the corpse concerning daily affairs while at the same time continuing to wail.
>
> After they had tied him into a fetal position, they got a large pot. Then they got another pot to use as a lid. In order to put the dead man on the fire they put him in the large pot with lots of water. Covering it with the other pot, they finished covering it. Then, they went to cut down two papaya trunks and returned with them. To stabilize the two pots, they set a papaya trunk deep into the earth on opposite sides, crossed them over the top, and lashed them together with vines. After they had done that, the pots remained secure [the bottom pot was pointed and sat in a small depression in the earth].
>
> Then they cut firewood, cutting large pieces the size of corner posts. In the surrounding gardens they repeatedly cut

firewood and brought it into the center of the communal house where they made a large pile. After they had piled the firewood, they took it and stuck it up on end leaning against the large pot, putting the firewood all around about four or five layers deep. Then they brought burning pieces of firewood and stuck them in among the others. While fanning the flames, they wailed all night in order to make medicine [magic]. They cooked it until dawn without sleeping.

Having wailed all night, now with the sun streaming through the side of the house, they pulled the firewood away and put out the remaining flames with water. With that done using leaves they swept the dirt floor all around the pot. While women were doing that, the men boiled bananas in order to eat them together with the flesh. Taking them off the fires, everyone was taking them off their various fires; they finished taking the boiled bananas off the cook fires.

It had fully dawned and the light was getting better, when a ceremonialist said to them, "We intend to eat. All of you come to the cooling pot." The men gathered, joined elbows and then by passing their right foot behind their left foot, they danced around the pot while it was cooling. Making the body cool, the ceremonialist had them sing the "send-the-spirit-away" rite/dance by chanting:

"Cool! Cool! Cool! Heee! Heee!
Let's eat! Let's eat! Let's eat!" he led them.

They repeated each stanza after him while shuffle-dancing and chanting. He continued:

"Ii ii, ii ii, ii ii,
Let's eat! Eat! Eat!
The tapir they brought which died, eat eat!
Tapir Child eat! Tapir Child eat!
His vegetables in the mouth mixing, eat!
His flesh in the mouth mixing,
His flesh in the mouth mixing,
Tapir Child eat! Tapir Child eat!
Being spirit-sending ones, eat!
Tapir Child eat!
His vegetables in mouth mix!
His flesh in mouth mix!
His vegetables in mouth mix!
His corn in mouth mix!
His flesh in mouth mix!

His vegetables in mouth mix!
Being spirit-sending ones
  his flesh in mouth mix!
His vegetables in mouth mix!
His cassava in mouth mix!
His flesh in mouth in mix!
His taro in mouth mix!
Being spirit-sending ones
  his flesh in mouth mix!
His vegetables in mouth mix!
His peanuts in mouth mix!
His *sacha camotes* in mouth mix!
Tapir Child eat!
All of you, eat! All of you, eat!
His sweet potatoes in mouth mix!
Do it! Do it! Do it! Do it!
Eat! Eat! Eat! Eat!
His dale dales in mouth mix!
His flesh in mouth eat!
His vegetables in mouth mix!
His sweet potatoes in mouth mix!
Having done so, finishing, do it!"

Thus, they finished dancing/chanting.

Then his people uncovered the pot, laid out a new palm leaf mat, and took out the body. After they had laid it out on the mat, many men [sic] variously said, "His thigh may I take? His arm may I take? His head may I take? Even I, his head may I take?" As they spoke, they took. Another ripped off his ribs. Another took his backbone. They did so to his entire body.

After repeatedly taking handfuls of boiled bananas, the men grouped here and there all around in order to eat his flesh and were eating. They mixed the boiled bananas with his flesh in their mouths while chewing. Continually eating, they finished it.

Gathering his bones, all of his bones gathering, going all around taking away his bones from them, his close relatives made a complete collection. Then breaking the covering pot, they divided it in two. Loading them into the pot halves, they gathered all the bones together. Then in order to converse, they again gathered in groups here and there in the communal house.

After having talked for awhile, they gathered all the partially burned firewood and rekindled the fire at the central hearth. After the flames were coming up in good fashion, wanting to toast the bones in order to soften them, they set the pot halves full of bones on the fire.

The men were still grouped here and there, so the ceremonialist called them together again and had them join elbows around the fire. And so that the little children would hook elbows with the older men and make medicine by doing the "send-the-spirit-away" rite/dance, the ceremonialist said, "Little children! With them shuffle your feet!" Then going around with them, the ceremonialist continued the "send-the-spirit-away" rite, chanting,

"Shrimp, guard his spirit!
Shrimp, guard his spirit!
Armored fish, guard his spirit!
Armored fish, guard his spirit!"

Having done that, he continued, chanting,

"Bones of one who can climb a rainbow are burning,
Bones of a very powerful one are burning,
Bones of one from the sky are burning,
Bones of saber-toothed tiger are burning,
Over very hard wood rainbow climber's bones are
   burning,
Those are burning,
Over very hard wood those are burning,
Rainbow climber's bones are burning,
Those are burning.
The flames are pushing out all over,
The flames are going good after almost dying,
The flames are moving all around."

After having done that, the ceremonialist separated the dead man's name, chanting:

"His hunting trails are overgrown,
His defecating place is overgrown,
His urinating place is overgrown,
His place of habitation is disassociated from him."

Having done that, he spoke to the dead man's spirit, chanting:

"You are a hawk.
You are a hummingbird.

> Don't be a blue hummingbird.
> When you meet the Inka Spirit,
>   by means of him go!
> To the Ancient Ones go!
> Not intending to come here again,
>   to them go!
> Inka body ornaments get rid of!
> Your seed cross-chest ornaments get rid of!
> To the Ancient Ones go!"

Then going, the dead man's spirit left.

After they had done that, they ended the ritual. Then in order to powder the bones, his wife put them in a mashing trough and began crushing them with a rocker pestle; powdering them she made them into a fine powder. Giving to her people, into all their little bowls she gave some of his powdered bones, she continually gave all around. Going with the bone powder, each one going to their place, to their section of the communal house they went. The next morning, after they had slept, everyone awoke. Then each woman reground the bone powder with food, like corn or peanuts in her mashing trough.

When that was done, the communal leader ordered them, "So that we can mix the bone powder with other food, go hunt game animals!" After he did that, all the men took their bows and arrows and went. While hunting game, killing armadillos, killing peccaries, killing turkey like *paujiles*, killing spider monkeys, killing partridges, collecting tortoises, they got lots of meat. Continually bringing it in, they brought the meat in all night long.

In the morning when all had awakened, all the women began boiling the meat until they had cooked it into a very soupy mush. Then they mixed in the powder that contained the dead man's bone powder and they all started drinking it. All the men drinking it, all the women drinking it, all the children drinking it, by drinking it they finished off the bone powder completely. Then the women continued wailing around the ashes where the body had been cooked, wailing until they had finished thinking of him. That is how they used to eat bodies long ago.

Pudicho gave me this account when I asked him about the "send-the-spirit-away" song that my translation assistant had told me was still being used. After the two short opening sentences, this entire account is told in one long continuous sentence with the quotation marks indicating embedded sentences. He did not use a reportative and I remember asking him whether he had ever eaten human flesh; a question he simply did not answer. I learned later from others that the eating of the dead ceased during the catastrophic epidemics of the late 1940s and early 1950s. There were too many bodies and everyone was too ill to participate.

The eating of the body was a duty performed out of respect and fear, as well as to gain the dead person's powers. Everything that had belonged to the person was gone. Even his/her name was disassociated from the spirit, so that the spirit would have no reason to stay around and haunt the close relatives. His garden was completely dug up and eaten. His weapons and tools were destroyed. His hunting trails, secret defecating place, and urinating place were avoided and left to be over-grown by the jungle. If it had been a woman it would have been the same, except she had no hunting trails. But the clay things she had made, her hammock, weaving paraphernalia, and her skirts would have been destroyed so as not to give her spirit any reason to remain. The entire ritual is intended to send the dead person's spirit to the ancestors and is finished by drinking the last remnant—his or her powdered bones.

5

Renewing Contact with Outsiders

After the Cashinahua men and women had adjusted to living in isolation without outsider things, they still longed for the objects that had changed their and their parent's lives. Pudicho tells the following.

> 38. Since their fathers had made the outsiders dangerous by shooting them, they lived in fear of them and since they had no guns, they could not raid to get things. So they remained not being able to get things, moving about hidden in the jungle, not killing anyone. However, by not accomplishing anything, they were suffering privation.

During those twenty or so years while they remained hidden, all the men, whom we later knew as adults, grew up and qualified to join a family as a son-in-law. Belisario, Pudicho's youngest brother, tells what it was like in those years.

> Later when my father had died and I was by myself, I had to make my own arrows. However, when I started I did it wrong; when I inserted the hard palm wood points into the cane shafts I seldom got it right. I tried to make the three-pronged fishing arrows and got it wrong. I then tried to make a bow properly and did it poorly. While suffering and wanting to weep over this learning process, I thought, "This is how one has to do it when one suffers and grows up without a father to teach us to work, and to hunt, and to tell stories, and to teach us all the things that we need to know in

order to live." I am telling you how I was growing up without a father and about how I got by; listen closely.

Thus, as I have been telling you, when I was by myself without a father, other men—various village leaders—said to me, "One can do the work this way." While doing that kind of work, while watching I got the idea; by thinking in my head I completely got the correct knowledge. Doing it like that I started hunting and making gardens on my own. My older brother [Pudicho] repeatedly helped me to do it correctly by making his garden adjoining mine and showing me how to do my planting. When I started, he kept saying, "This is how one is able to do it. Do it this way. Our father always did it this way," by doing this he taught me. In this manner I made gardens, hunted, and did all various kinds of things that a man does, gaining maturity from my brother's instruction.

When my people saw this, they arranged for me to take a wife. One of my paternal aunts saw all that I was doing and made me her son-in-law by having me take her daughter as a wife. After that I worked for her household, not being at all lazy. They were saying, "Our nephew is not able to be lazy. He makes garden for us; he cuts firewood for us; he builds for us; when the village goes to drug fish with poison, he gets fish for us; after he has planted his garden, he plants cotton for us and when it is time to spin it, he makes spindles for us. And when we want to weave hammocks, he makes the loom parts for us out of black palm wood. By liking us and being agreeable to our requests, our nephew is able to be very helpful for us."

By means of the same knowledge I always do these same things for my wives now.

Because Belisario was such a good worker and hunter he was also given a second daughter as a wife. This was to insure that he would stay with that family group until he was securely attached to his wives and children. And even though they were able to raise a new generation and to make a living, the Cashinahua in Peru still wanted the manufactured things they remembered their parents having. Belisario tells about an early attempt to make a contact.

When I was almost grown up, the first of our grown men made a frustrated effort to go and see the outsiders, but they became frightened of the outsider sicknesses and ran away.

Renewing Contact with Outsiders

At first when they went downriver, they followed the river's edge, like animals, without canoes; they did not have anything by which to go on the water, so they made a canoe out of a palm tree trunk and a raft to go and try to get metal tools. We were like animals without metal tools; we were like animals without mosquito nets; and we were like animals without clothes. Intending to get clothes, mosquito nets, machetes, and axes, they went downriver but each one got to thinking, "If I do not have the outsiders' words, they might kill me." Because of this they returned empty-handed following the edge of the river. I saw that when I was a teenager.

This fearful attitude was not shared, however, by all the leaders. Pudicho tells how an older brother, who was probably a classificatory brother, took courage to make contact.

39. Then while an airplane was flying over, my aged older brother, who owned the harpy eagle feather costume as a sign of leadership, proposed making contact with the outsiders, saying, "That sky motor is flying by going downriver taking supplies to the outsiders' villages. We are suffering privation. Our children also are suffering because we are not able to make the things they need. I intend to make contact with the outsiders and get axes, machetes, and shooters—outsider guns—for them."

But another leader said, "Don't make contact! Don't make contact! Our fathers made them very angry and dangerous, they could shoot us! Don't contact those whom they made dangerous just a few years ago."

But my older brother, realizing that he could do it, said, "I will not refrain from making contact with them. I will start a peaceful relationship." He knew that the spirit Sky Trail, that had entered him long ago, had bitter medicine and would now blow on the outsiders for him to pacify them. So he and another leader, each with a son, came downriver and showed themselves to outsiders.

40. Another indigenous group, the Yaminahua, were settled there to cut logs and collect rubber. My older brother also unintentionally met a real outsider, but the Yaminahua frightened them by saying, "You're the ones who always war with Yamis!" Being afraid, they went upstream to their home and after arriving in the village, my older brother said to the

men, "I am returning from making contact with the Yaminahua. Those outsiders are coming, don't club them and don't shoot them. We are suffering without tools, without knives, machetes, axes, guns, and clothing. After they shot the outsiders during the first contact, our fathers brought us over here with clothing long ago. Those clothes wore out long ago and we have to wear vine or cotton penis straps. So that we can again wear proper clothing, don't try to shoot these people, any of you! And you, young men, don't you try to shoot them either! I am making peaceful contact with them." In that way he prohibited them.

This was not the first airplane they had seen. They tell about the first time an airplane or "sky motor" flew low over one of their houses and they shot arrows at it. Now they chuckle about that incident, but back then it was a recognition that they could not remain hidden and that there were things to be obtained downriver.

Leadership is not hereditary. A capable man with charismatic qualities can become the coordinator of a communal group; they even tell of a woman who once became a leader. In those early days a leader was required to be well-versed in all the communal ceremonies and rites, and to possess the macaw and harpy eagle feathers used in making the *chidin* rite costume. An aspiring leader would listen closely to all the ceremonies, and seek the help of relatives and friends to collect the needed feathers. Obtaining these and a leader's woven cape or tunic, made by the women, established acceptance as a possible leader. Today, personal documents, being able to read and write, and competence in dealing with the outside world is more important.

After Pudicho's older brother's return, he tells his people that he has made arrangements for the real outsider to visit, and he feels it necessary to exhort the group to act peaceably if they want to obtain trade goods on a continuous basis. The story continues as follows.

> 41. Later while he was still prohibiting them, those outsiders were approaching. Those Yaminahua invited my older brother, who had previously gone to visit them, to come out to meet them and accompanied him into the village. Then the real outsider [Mr. Sutano], who was bringing the Yaminahua, had everybody go into the communal house. Then when my people were about to give them presents, the Yaminahua all said, "Give me things. Cause me to grasp things."
>
> In order to give them things, the Genuine men were thinking, "What shall I give them?" They gave them teeth necklaces—a great quantity of necklaces—oriole tail feather

headdresses, trumpeter down headdresses, and they also gave them baby carriers to wear as headdresses. And then they took manufactured things in trade from the Yaminahua.

42. After they did that and as the outsiders were leaving, the Genuine men wanted to kill them to get the rest of their things. But because my older brother again prohibited our people, the outsiders were able to go safely back downstream. While the outsiders were going, the Genuine men still wanting to get more things, followed them on foot all the way to their houses, where the Yaminahua threatened them with guns chasing them away. Being afraid, they returned home by following the stream's edge all night, not knowing that they had contracted the outsider sickness influenza. As the sickness was spreading, the ancient ones who were very old and various of their grown children and even their younger children were leaving their own children because the outsider sickness was causing them to die off.

The Cashinahua's great yearning for trade goods resulted in the first of six epidemics which almost exterminated the Genuine people from Peruvian territory. An example of the devastation and its consequences was given to me by Ana, who, though we had known her for twenty-five years, was not willing to speak to a tape recorder until 1994. She relates those times in the following.

By means of the outsider sickness my husband died. The outsider's dizziness sickness entered him and he was very feverish. When I lived on the Xapuya my husband died; next my child died, the child that my husband engendered died. When they contacted the outsiders, the outsiders' sickness infected them and then the Marinahua (Yaminahua) brought the sickness, and the child of my first pregnancy died. Then the sickness killed the second child that I had conceived, a male child. Finally, it did the same thing to the other child that I had conceived; I was living without children.

Then your brother took me long ago. When your brother asked me if he could continually sexually penetrate me, I said, "I am not making anyone to be a husband. I do not want to make you my husband. I do not want to sit as two with my sister [who was already his wife]. I will not sit with my sister. Besides, I hear that she does not want to share her husband."

> Not listening to me, he made me his wife and made a child in me long ago; he made a female child which the outsiders' sickness entered, making her weaken and die long ago. Then he gave me another child but I lost the pregnancy. Next he gave me my Roberto and after he was born and growing, I brought him here and then I conceived Francisco. After I conceived him, bloody diarrhea got a hold of me and I was suffering when Ken [Kensinger] returned and made me well. After I was up and about and we were living together, I conceived a female child: that woman Juliana over there. Juliana was the only girl I raised. That is all the children I have, the ones your namesake gave me.

This is from a woman who became happy to be the third wife in a three-wife household. She now has a married daughter to care for her in her old age and two fine sons, one of whom will probably be the next village leader in Balta. At the time Ana's first husband fell ill, many of the other Cashinahua wanted to flee, but Pudicho tells how he exerted himself.

> 43. While the influenza was making them die off, one of the men warned us fearfully, saying, "Let's flee! Just as our parents made us flee long ago, so we were told, let's get out of here!"
>
> While he repeatedly said that, I myself thought it over and said to them, "Let's not flee! Even though my older brother is an old man, he is making peaceful contact for us with the outsiders. We are frustrated in our desire to have guns and we have to shoot game with our bows and arrows. While suffering this privation, we have to work hard scraping the hard *pijuayo* palm wood to make bows and arrows. Let's not be afraid of the outsiders, so we can get guns from them and then we will have lots of meat to eat." After I said this, I continued peaceful contact with the outsiders.

Pudicho's younger brother Belisario had a little to add concerning the cause of the sickness.

> Okay, it was like this when my people started seeing the outsiders long ago. Because we did not have the outsider sicknesses long ago, we were living contentedly when the outsiders started making contact with us. They were coming and going with their sicknesses when my people got their sickness and almost completely died off, without anyone left;

> all my ancient relatives died. Not all of them died just of the outsider's sickness; we were told that the Yaminahua did us harm by burning medicine against us; burning black things, stabbing the smoke with needles, causing pain in our people as they died; it did not touch the people like influenza does, it touched everybody as they were dying long ago. Some were dying and some of us were getting well; those of us who were left, we were then alive.

Pudicho had another brother, Idiodoro, who is older than Belisario. He helped me to understand their relationships with the various river traders. He has the following to say about his older brother's continued peaceful contact.

> We were living on the Xapuya [a side stream of the Curanja]. It was like this when Mr. Sutano came to meet us long ago. Wanting to make them work, he went to our people to contact them and make them accustomed to him so he could make them work; then he took some of them with him long ago. After he came and lived with them, he took them downstream and made them accustomed to him by giving them a few things and a few clothes in order to make them work. Then when Mr. Sutano had them used to their new situation, he was the first to say to them, "Cut trees into logs so I can get things for you." Mr. Sutano was the first to get them started cutting logs long ago; but he only gave them a few things and left to move over to the Ucayali River.

Mr. Sutano worked for many years with the groups the Cashinahua call Yaminahua, who were at that time in the process of moving down the Curanja River in stages ahead of the Cashinahua. I had never heard of him until 1994, and inquired about him in Puerto Esperanza. His relatives told me that he was very much alive and retired in Atalaya on the Ucayali River. Mr. Sutano's contact with the Cashinahua must have been short or kept secret, because the next trader Dini Fulano, a Peruvian national who later made the first enduring contact, did not know of their existence when he made a peaceful but unexpected contact with the Cashinahua in about 1946 or 1947.

In 1994 at his house in Pucallpa, Dini Fulano told me the following.

> I left San Marcos with an Indian helper named Ixki. I don't remember the year. We went up the Purús River in a small canoe to the Curanja River to cut logs. I only took my shotgun with four shells, a machete, an axe, a crosscut saw, and

one sack of farina meal. On the lower part of the Curanja there were a lot of my people felling trees and taking out logs. After we had gotten out a few logs working with the other Peruvians, Ixki wanted to return home because there were so few good trees. But I wanted to go farther upstream to look for good trees near the edge of the river.

We then poled our canoe upstream until we reached the side stream Xapuya. I saw that it was a good stream coming in on the right-hand side of the Curanja River; it looked like it might have some good trees. At the mouth of this stream we made a small encampment with a raised platform on which to store our things and the small sack of farina meal. While we were at this camp we saw a small amount of smoke in the distance but we did not pay much attention to it.

We later poled up this stream a little ways and then began walking along the edge of the stream in search of good trees. While I was going along looking at the treetops, I lowered my eyes and right there in front of me stood an Indian with his bow fully drawn, with the arrow pointed directly at my chest. Immediately, others aimed their fully-drawn arrows at Ixki's chest also. Right away they relieved us of our things: shotgun, ax, machete, and saw. They took us captive at about 10 o'clock in the morning and made us walk upstream all day long until about five in the afternoon. As we climbed a hill covered with banana plants, we entered their village where there were a lot of men armed with bows and arrows, but we did not see any women.

They separated us, putting me in a large house by myself and Ixki in a different place. They brought me a new hammock and a little gruel to drink. The next day they gave me some food. I stayed there in that house alone for three days. Then they brought Ixki to where I was and tried to talk to us using a few words of Portuguese, identifying themselves as Cashinahua. By words and hand motions, I told them that we wanted to cut trees and take logs downriver. They understood and went downstream with us to cut trees. After we had cut lots of logs, we floated them down to the mouth of the stream where we secured them to wait for the water to rise in the main river. Then the Cashinahuas, who were with us, heard some monkeys in the distance and went off to shoot them, leaving only one of their group with us. Ixki and I looked at each other and said, "Let's go back downstream."

The one Cashinahua was willing to accompany us, so we took him back to San Marcos with us.

The next year I returned to the Xapuya with a canoe full of things to become a trader with the Cashinahua. Little by little they moved downstream on the Xapuya closer to where I could bring my supplies in a canoe. Finally, they came all the way down to the main river, the Curanja, and settled at Conta, where I continued to trade with them.

The Cashinahua men told me that Ixki, the man who accompanied Fulano, was a *Nixinawa* 'Vine outsider' and that they knew him in subsequent years. His language was of the same family (Panoan) as theirs. But due to variations in grammar and lack of familiarity with his pronunciation, the Cashinahua men had some difficulty communicating with him and were probably limited to individual words and phrases.

Then, as well as today, the frontier Peruvians were able to adapt themselves very well to the jungle, living off the land much as the indigenous people did. Fulano and Ixki traveled light because in the dry season the water is shallow. It probably took them one long dawn-to-dusk day of poling to reach the mouth of the Curanja River from San Marcos. Then after they left the lower Curanja where they had been cutting trees, it would have taken them one week or more of all-day poling to reach the mouth of the side stream Xapuya. They were looking for *cedro*, a smooth-grained wood which is related to mahogany, and *espingo*, an oak-like wood which has long been in demand downriver in Brazil. Logs are one of the few natural products easy to extract with simple tools, especially when the marketable trees are near a stream that will flood enough in the rainy season to float out the logs.

I still remember Dini Fulano telling me of seeing the fully-drawn bow pointed at his chest. Even at 79, sitting in the humble parlor of his retirement home, he became agitated, widened his eyes, and raised his hands as he told me of his fright. After the Cashinahua took Fulano and Ixki to their village at the headwaters of the Xapuya and separated them, they talked for three days trying to decide whether to kill him. Fulano did not have the advantage of having many indigenous guards to protect him as Mr. Sutano had had when he visited that village. Araguana, Pudicho's sister's husband, told me that he had to physically restrain his father to prevent him from killing the outsider. Pudicho and the others, however, who wanted to establish trade, prevailed and helped Fulano and Ixki cut logs. By the time Dini Fulano had returned the following year, the price of wild rubber had risen again such that it was more profitable than logs and easier to market.

Concerning their relations with the river traders, Pudicho's brother Idiodoro remembers the following.

> After Mr. Sutano left, then Dini contacted us and said, "I also, I will make you work. Collect rubber. If you work getting rubber I will give you things."
>
> However, when we collected rubber he mistreated us by hardly giving us anything. When he gave us only a small amount of things, he would say, "You must pay. You haven't finished paying for the things yet. Go collect more!"
>
> While we were working with him, he continued mistreating us; when there was a 50-kilo ball of rubber sitting on the ground, he would say, "It is 10 kilos." By vainly hefting it with his hands, he would say, "It is only 10 kilos. Do another 10 kilos," and then he gave us only a small piece of soap. When he gave us small quantities of things, he always said, "Get more and I will bring you more things. Get more!" However, when he didn't bring us things he was making us suffer privation.
>
> Then the Yaminahua Alfonso criticized the outsider saying, "He is mistreating you. Do as I tell you," and then he started teaching us some of the outsiders' words. By using his own language Alfonso taught my brother Belisario and your namesake a few of the outsiders' words. [My namesake is Grompes, referred to as my brother, the leader in Balta in 1975.]

As Pudicho continues his story, he tells of Dini Fulano's attempt to solidify his hold on their group.

> 44. Then an outsider, whom I myself had pacified, established a parent-like relationship with my son, a child that I engendered, and dealt with him as if he were the leader of our group. This caused my son to think, "I am the son of a headman and I, too, intend to be a leader." Treating him as the leader of our group, the outsider repeatedly gave him things and took him to visit downriver.

This may have been the time when Pudicho's son acquired his outsider name, Grompes. The traders needed names to label each man in order to keep their accounts straight, and the Genuine men did not easily reveal their Genuine names. And even if they had, the traders would have found them difficult to pronounce and even harder to write. So every adult man, including Pudicho, began to be labeled with an Hispanic name, something which has now become a part of the face they show to the outside world. Dini Fulano may have been impressed with the bit of Spanish Pudicho's son Grompes was learning and recognized him as a future leader. Having known Pudicho, I doubt he was impressed, even though the boy was his own son. Pudicho was a stouthearted leader, as he states in the next section.

> 45. About this same time, those of my people, who had not escaped with my Ancient Ones long ago, again made peaceful contact with the Brazilians; the Genuine people were living among them and working for them. Hearing that they were collecting rubber and *seringue* and getting many things, most of the Genuine people, who were on this side [Curanja], went over to the Embira River to where they had made contact, to see for themselves. I was told that they were going because they said that they wanted to live in peace and were afraid that the outsiders on this side might shoot them. However, my heart remained strong. By pacifying the outsiders I had come to the point of dwelling peaceably with them. And even though I was vulnerable to being shot by the Yaminahua, I remained steadfast in my decision to stay on the side stream Xapuya.
>
> At that time my older brother was continuing to contact the outsiders for me. He was getting many things for our people: guns, cloth, mosquito nets, and other things. Then my people were no longer eating out of clay bowls; they didn't cook in and eat from clay pots. They were cooking in metal pots and eating from metal bowls and plates; they were drinking their gruel from metal cups; together with my close relatives I lived with them.
>
> 46. Back then when the things were worn out and almost all gone, and my older brother had been contacting the outsiders for several months, my people were fearful; they had no place to go or escape. Pitying themselves, they feared the outsiders, saying, "The outsiders might shoot us." But I was not afraid. I was not afraid of the outsiders' sicknesses. I was not afraid of dying. I was not afraid of being shot by the outsiders. When I went to dwell by the stream, I thought out loud, "I will dwell. By the water I will dwell." Thus, I descended to the large stream many years ago.

The Cashinahua refer to the area where the headwaters of the Juruá proper, the Tarauacá, the Embira, and the Curanja rivers rise in relative proximity to each other, as "the Center". This indicates the area in which their ancestors had lived as foot Indians. Crossing this area on foot from north to south, staying on the uplands to avoid the larger streams, may take several weeks or slightly more than a month if the men are accompanied by women and children carrying limited household goods while the men forage for food. In the same way that Pudicho's group had edged down the Curanja, the children of their relatives, who had escaped with them, had edged down the Tarauacá and Embira rivers seeking things in Brazil. Communication between the Cashinahua on the two river systems, the Juruá and Purús, has been motivated by their desire to visit close relatives and by the desire of young men to seek another location for marriage if a local situation is not to their liking or they are not accepted by a household in their home community.

Even though Pudicho may have been tempted to return to the river of his birth, he told me of his determination, as a vigorous young man, to stay in the seemingly less advantageous situation on the Curanja River. Pudicho even becomes nostalgic, saying:

> 47. Before that I lived permanently up in the uplands where there are only small streams. And so that they could dance the *Chidin* with the large harpy eagle feathers and eat spider monkey heads, I got the monkey heads and gave them to my people. I also made the *kacha* log, and by giving them meat I celebrated with my people. That is how I used to live in the uplands.

The primary function of the *Chidin* dance/chant, in my experience, was to aid the spirit of an important dead man to reach the ancient ones. Kensinger reports that the *Chidin* rite was used to restore unity to the village when dissent threatened the social fabric (1995:176). Both the exchange of cooked spider monkey heads in the *Chidin* rite and the reciprocal giving of meat and drink at the *Kacha* ceremony were carried out between male cross-cousins. This was a sign of group solidarity and acknowledgment of reciprocal responsibilities.[8]

Pudicho now tells of the move that changed his life.

> 48. It was from there in the uplands that my older brother contacted the outsiders for me and I descended to live by the water long ago. After I descended to the stream [Xapuya] to

---

[8]For more information on *Chidin*, headman's rite, and *Kachanawa*, fertility rite, see Kensinger (1995:Index—Rituals and Rites).

make a garden, I cleared and burned a garden plot and then planted my crops; I planted cassava, bananas, and all manner of garden plants. While eating from that garden, I built a house. That's how my life was when I had descended to live by the large side stream long ago.

This was a strategic move in his life and in the lives of his group. They were making the transition from being foot Indians to being river Indians, which would entail many conceptual changes and the learning of new skills. It was a change they did not find easy, as Belisario relates.

Now I will tell you how we lived when the outsiders first contacted us and how we suffered like animals to get their things. They did not give us anything for free; it was by means of our work, our work at collecting rubber, that we started to get things. We cut down the trees and collected the hardened sap but we did not know how much weight a kilo of rubber was or its value. Because we did not yet know anything, we suffered like animals; almost for free we worked rubber to our detriment; for a little amount of salt we collected rubber; for a few clothes we constantly collected rubber.

We were using only bows and arrows, as the ancient ones had taught us, to shoot animals in order to eat meat. We knew how difficult it was to shoot peccary and tapir with an arrow when we made contact with the outsiders. But we really suffered when we saw them shooting off their guns all over the place. However, we learned, and got guns from them long ago. I got my first gun from Dini, from an outsider named Dini. I got my first gun which was very expensive, and even though it was very expensive, I got it and paid for it with rubber. I paid for it for many months and by means of it I shot game and we ate meat. At that time, that outsider Dini was the only outsider living downriver from whom we got things. However, later lots of outsiders came over from the other side [Ucayali Valley] to make contact with us; they let each of us have a shotgun while making us work.

In addition to the metal tools that they needed to work the jungle, Belisario expresses the value of a shotgun to their way of life. Even though most of the grown men were expert with a bow and arrow and could call most of the game animals into range, they are not nostalgic when comparing the two weapons. In his thinking at that time, the shotgun's effectiveness made it well worth Belisario's months of labor to pay for it.

The outside world of Peru has always tried to limit the supply of both guns and ammunition to the indigenous people. This is done by setting high prices and creating bureaucratic complications. Because the government does not want armed challenges to their authority, they limit hunting weapons to 16-gauge shotguns and allow only BB shot, which is not effective against people at any significant distance. Buckshot or slugs are more effective for killing the large game animals. Twenty-two caliber rifles would serve well for most of their hunting, including deer, and would be less expensive, but the .22 ammunition, powerful enough for hunting are difficult to obtain.

Theoretically, any indigenous man could buy a shotgun, but would have to travel to a city where shotguns are sold and where there is a Civil Guard office that issues licenses. To obtain a license he also needs personal documents showing that he is a Peruvian citizen. Birth registers and personal documents were not readily available to the indigenous people in the Purús region until the 1980s. In addition, a person wanting to purchase shotgun shells wholesale in a city, until a few years ago, had to get a license from the Civil Guard. Fortunately, during the years we worked with the Cashinahua, I had Ministry of Education documents and made acquaintances at the Civil Guard office in Pucallpa, so I bought shotgun shells wholesale in cases of 500 shells each. Being acquainted at the Civil Guard office was necessary to get the paperwork moved along; otherwise, it could sit for a week or more. I never bought shotguns in someone else's name, but I always helped the Cashinahua men who came in to study to get their personal documents and assisted them through the gun purchase licensing process. The school teachers soon learned to do it on their own, but the ordinary person living out in the border areas needed intermediaries to handle the process on their behalf. Thus, hunting for skins—primarily alligator, peccary, deer, nutria, ocelot, and jaguar—became the principal economic resource in the Purús region in the 1960s. The river traders, who came from other parts of Peru, made sure their clients had shotguns and ammunition. They were able to obtain ammunition by verifying to the Civil Guard that they had many clients. The system, however, obliged them to use personal influence with the Civil Guard and the name of a person other than the client, who was not present, in order to obtain the license necessary to buy a shotgun for each client.

6
An Unequal Situation

Pudicho again picks up the story referring to Dini Fulano's early rubber collecting trips, but centers on being exploited for his food crops.

49. After I had settled by the stream, an outsider was thinking of me and went upriver to get my garden produce, which was not to my advantage. He came repeatedly and got my cassava, my sugar cane, my fresh corn and my papaya; he did this to my detriment by giving me only a few things in payment. That's how I was living when the Yaminahua took me downriver many years ago.

50. Back when my people were afraid and fled to Brazil months before, these same Yaminahua said to me, "We are moving so we can work for the outsiders. Move downstream for the time being"; then they gave me the land they had been living on further down the Xapuya [With-Cotton] side stream. I worked to possess it by making a garden. The Yaminahua had said to me, "Make your garden here!" So I cleared all the underbrush, felled the trees, and burned it after everything was thoroughly dried. After I had planted them months before, my crops were growing correctly; because it wanted to, my cassava was maturing steadily. Then, when the *yukan* trees were in full bloom, I planted peanuts on the stream bank.

Dini Fulano was a *patrón,* an overseer boss who normally thought he was doing the Indians a service by acting as a go-between to do for them what they could not do for themselves. And in this position he had a combination of a proprietary and patronizing attitude. Thus, Fulano felt that low-cost food to feed his own family was his due as compensation for the two-week or so round trip he made each month or so to visit them. The Cashinahua can subtly make an ordinary statement into a detrimental one by adding a nasal or nasalized vowel to the verb in a clause. This is what Pudicho did, but also made sure I understood by stressing the fact of the low payment. Still, he was the leader of the group, and so felt he had to placate the outsider Dini so that he would continue to come with the trade goods they valued so highly.

When making a garden, the Cashinahua men are very careful to chop all the brush and limbs down to within two feet of the ground so that after it dries it will yield a good clean burn, eliminating all grass and weeds. And because the topsoil which contains all the insect life is only three or four inches deep, a good hot burn will eliminate the majority of the insect larvae that would attack the roots of the crops. This is done during the sunny dry season, July and August, so that Pudicho would have had his new crop of cassava by the following April or May when the *yukan* trees were in bloom, a signal to plant peanuts and corn down by the rivers and streams. The flowering of various trees provides them with a natural calendar for planting at various locations. If he had planted his peanuts too soon, a late rain could flood the streams and wash away all his work.

Even though Pudicho had been resolute about staying on the Curanja drainage in Peru when most of his people went to Brazil seeking manufactured things, news of plenty in Brazil made him waver, as he tells here.

> 51. After I had the peanuts planted, I heard that our people had made peaceful contact on the Embira River and were getting a great quantity of things. "They are getting things for free without paying money. By just working they are getting lots of things, so I was told," someone was telling me. Because of this Genuine man's report, I became interested and went over there many years ago.

> 52. Crossing over the uplands we descended to the Embira River and traveling downstream we came to where my people dwelt. They were living around a Brazilian boss named Pedro, who managed their lives. But after I made contact with them, they were unwilling to share the opportunity to work for him, so my son [Grompes] spoke to me, saying, "Father! Having made that outsider boss to be their owner, they are withholding him from us. Let's go downriver and make a

different boss our owner." Having said this, he took me on downriver long ago.

As he took me downriver, I met a bad boss, who caused us to stay with him, saying, "Make a garden for me." After we had made a garden for him, he became abusive; by drinking rum and talking a lot, he was acting in a frightening manner. Being afraid, my wife said to me, "Why did you bring me over here? On the other side we had made goodness our owner. On the other side [Curanja], my aged cousin made peaceful contact for us with the Peruvian outsiders months ago! I, I am afraid of this Brazilian! Let's go back again!" By doing this she was thinking for me; a woman actually thought. Rejecting the Brazilian, and returning, I brought them to this side [Curanja].

53. Coming upriver, we crossed back over to this side. Then the Peruvians, who were making others collect rubber for them, met me at my house and said, "Where have you gone and are returning from?"

I said, "I went and visited my people. From visiting my people, I am returning."

They then told me, "Collect rubber for us. Then we will give you mosquito nets, blankets, cloth, and axes. Work for us."

So I began to collect rubber, and in exchange for a large bundle of rubber I got a machete and they gave me an axe. Working with those I lived.

The recurring theme in Pudicho's account is their desire to obtain manufactured things and his trip to Brazil shows the good and the bad aspects of the patrón system. When an outsider boss is good from their point of view, it leaves the indigenous people free to work the rain forest that they know best. When they can get the things they need and are unable to make, the work they put in may not seem excessive to them. But many bosses have acted as sovereigns, demanding production from them and by agreement with other bosses, exclusive access to the group's labor while keeping them in constant debt (Hemming 1987:247–248, 252–253, 293).

During this same time period Pudicho's cross-cousin Araguana made a trip downriver which demonstrated their cultural isolation and brought on another epidemic which further reduced their population. He tells it in the following.

Being ignorant of what was downriver, not yet knowing, I was traveling in that direction. I did not go by means of a real canoe, but rather I was going in a *pona* palm canoe. I had collected rubber and was going with my cross-cousins to see the outsiders. We did not yet know how to control a canoe; one of our people said, "I myself, I know," so we took him with us. When he was taking us, he did not know how to pole a canoe, so we were going in all different directions, hitting the river banks. Zig-zagging down the river, we got turned around at a deep hole and nosed into a beach. We really suffered as we continued downriver and then slept on a beach. We kept going and sleeping on beaches.

Finally, we entered among the Yaminahua. We did not know anything so they cheated us. Because we had not yet learned any outsiders' words, they completely took our rubber, to our detriment. After that the Yaminahua took the canoe we were using, even though I said, "Don't take it. You took my rubber away from me yesterday. Don't take the canoe," they took it away from us and left. We were in a pitiable state when the Yaminahua named Sakadia came and ordered us to take his canoe, saying, "Do you know how to pole a canoe?"

We said, "We do not know."

Then he pointed to another man and said, "This one knows how to pole a canoe," and that other man took us downriver. After we had entered the outsiders' village we went into Dini's house and asked for things. Thinking of the rubber we had brought, he only gave us a few machetes and some shirts. We slept there and because we laid around there for two nights, the influenza got us. After the influenza got us, we were suffering and left Sakadia's canoe behind. We walked up alongside the river until we arrived at his village. His people said, "Why didn't you bring his canoe? When you fellows came here several days ago, we took your hammocks and your bows and arrows. And then he gave you his canoe to use. Why didn't you bring it back?"

We finally said to them, "We were unknowing when we came the other day. When we came back, we didn't bring the canoe that Sakadia loaned to us, because we were sick."

However, it was because of the influenza we brought from there that our people died. Our brothers died; our women died; and our parents died of outsiders' sickness long ago.

Being ignorant we brought the influenza that killed my children and my parents.

After people stopped dying, we who survived the trip finally told the others, "We did not understand canoes, so we walked along the river's edge and were constantly falling in the water. Suffering, we entered the village." They all laughed and made fun of us. Then someone suggested out loud, "Let's again collect rubber." We again felled the rubber trees and collected their juice after we slashed the bark. Later when someone took a load of rubber downriver to Esperanza, he returned sick. He returned and caused our people to suffer a great deal of pain; our grown adults were dying off; it entered me also and I was dying, when someone made me swallow a lot of medicine. After I swallowed a lot of medicine, someone stabbed me with a needle and I got better; I was able to stand up. I also almost died and they treated me and I got better. However, even though the same ones made them swallow medicine, many of my people died on me. My older brother died; my wife died; my older sister died; my nephews died; and my children died. Then my paternal aunt left me dying; my cross-cousin died. That quantity of my people all died on me; I, only I got better and lived.

After I got better, I wanted to move downriver and said, "Let's go downriver. Because lots of our people have died here at this location, let's move downriver. Let's settle downriver near the outsiders." So we came in stages, moving our houses every few years and finally we arrived and settled at Conta [on the Curanja River].

Again, they paid a high price for contact, but this time there was no talk of running away. Araguana's wife, who died in those early epidemics, was not Pudicho's sister Louisa, who was also Araguana's co-wife at that time. He had two more co-wives later, whom we also knew. Later, when we treated them during an influenza epidemic, they identified it as the same sickness that killed their relatives in the past. Araguana also told me that it was the man from San Paulo who caused him to swallow the medicine. Belisario told of the same visit by these different outsiders as follows.

> Thus, when we had become a bit accustomed to the Peruvian outsiders, a different outsider boss came from downriver; from very far downriver a big boss left San Paulo and came to examine us. After he arrived he wrote down our leader's words, asking for them using our Genuine words,

which he had learned while coming upriver. Hearing him use our words, our people were very happy, thinking, "One of our Genuine people has come. He is not an outsider; he is a Genuine person." Being very happy, they told him various different types of our Ancient Ones' words and about the many different implements we used to make back then. However, as he spoke his own words with those who had come with him, we were thinking, "He talks completely different, in a way we have never heard. He can't be an outsider like the Brazilians and Peruvians. He is a Genuine person."

Because my people were so very happy with them, they had them make a new canoe for them, giving them things and taking pictures of them. While they were living with my people, they gave them all types of things without asking payment. Then when they left, they took our big leader Kanamadeti [also named Napoleon] with them to visit downriver. And then as they were leaving to enter Brazil, their boss gave him two shotguns and said, "I can come again," but he did not return and I heard that he has died.

When we were translating Belisario's recording in 1994, Pudicho's son Grompes told me that he also remembered that group's visit. He said that the group consisted of four of the different outsiders, three Neanahuas, and four Genuine men. He remembered that the leader of the group was named Adolfo, who was a little bit old with white in his beard and that he gave him some fishhooks. There was also a secretary named Roy, who wrote down their answers to the questions. In addition there was Geraldo, who took pictures (Schultz 1962), and another helper whose name he had forgotten. Grompes also reported that they stayed about a month but that Napoleon was only deceiving them when he claimed to be a paramount leader. The only paramount leader he ever knew of was Chanemaiti, who led the revolt and escaped from Brazil and whom Grompes remembers seeing as a very young child.

This little talk with Grompes helped me tremendously to put a few Western dates to this story. We had previously, in the early 1970s, estimated that he and I were about the same age. This was all further clarified by learning about the visit of the group from San Paulo in 1951, as noted by the anthropological photographer Harald [Geraldo] Schultz (1955:182). Grompes said that they arrived soon after Maria and he had started living together which was not too long after he had gone through puberty. Thus, he was born in the late 1930s.

Fortunately, a report of this expedition was published in the magazine of the *Museu Paulista* of San Paulo; the portion concerning the trip up the Curanja River follows.

> Upriver from the side stream Conta, to the east of the Purús, is its tributary, the Curanja River. From the mouth of the Curanja, it takes nine days' poling upstream to reach the first village of Kachinaua Indians. We came across eight villages in all; the number of inhabitants per village ranged between 20 and 120. We calculated that the total number of Kachinaua was between 450 and 500.
>
> Their first contact with Peruvians had been about five or six years before, when a group of Kachinaua Indians appeared at the mouth of the Curanja River. Accompanied by a group of Peruvians, the Indians went back to their villages demonstrating themselves to be peaceful and desirous of entering into commerce with the civilized ones.
>
> Since this first contact, an increasing number of Kachinaua men have devoted themselves to the extraction of *caucho* rubber and cutting logs. At various times Peruvian and Brazilian merchants have made the painful trip up the Curanja River to trade with them. As a result of contact with our civilization they have acquired measles, which killed the majority of the women in the first village.
>
> The villages are made up of several houses. Their open structure is rectangular, built with posts and beams and covered by a two-sided leaf roof that reaches nearly to the ground. In some villages, in addition to the Kachinaua-style houses, there are others on posts, with floors made of slit *paxiuba* palm bark. These are identical to the houses of the civilized residents on the Alto Purús that were constructed—so say the Indians—to house the loggers and rubber collectors. The houses of primitive construction are large, attaining up to 40 meters in length and 10 to 12 meters in width.
>
> The Kachinaua of the Alto Curanja seem to have migrated from the tributaries of the Embira River, which is part of the Juruá basin. They have been there for one generation, or perhaps longer, because of a misunderstanding among the various groups. The others stayed in their original region in Brazilian territory maintaining constant contact with the resident civilized ones. The Indians who migrated probably

followed the waters of the Alto Embira upstream and then entering the headwaters of the stream Chapuia, they were penetrating onto the Alto Curanja, a region occupied by the Jaminaua Indians and to this day they are their most lively felt enemy. The actual territory of the Kachinaua Indians is limited upriver by the first rapids where one encounters the first rocks and cliffs that do not exist downriver, nor on the entire length of the Purús River.

Today the Kachinaua, who live in the villages downriver from the side stream Chapuia, show a tendency to move down the Curanja River a little more each year, with the object of being near the Peruvians to facilitate trade. They do this in spite of fearing contact which they know causes them to lose numerous lives because of measles and other diseases. However, despite the great attraction metal tools have for them, the two villages located on the side stream Chapuia did not demonstrate the tendency to move toward the civilized ones, because they fear their illnesses.

The principal activities of the Kachinaua men are farming, hunting, and most recently the extraction of logs and *caucho* rubber. An imbalance is evident between the work load of the men and the women. The new metal tools, whether machetes, axes, or knives, greatly facilitate the cutting down and clearing of the forest and the making of weapons and utensils. This is in no way comparable to the work done by the women, who make their fired clay pots by the same traditional processes, manually spin and weave their cotton on the same primitive looms, and braid small baskets and mats from palm leaves, all in the traditional manner. Finally, concerning cooking, the only innovation is the use of a broken piece of knife blade to peel the cassava. The Kachinaua women work from early dawn to nightfall, while the men, who complete their activities more rapidly, remain in the village the rest of the day without anything to do....

We had the opportunity to read to the Indians passages from the excellent work by Capistrano do Abreu, *Ra-txa-huni-kui,* concerning the Kachinaua of the Embira River. They confirmed not only the accuracy of the annotations done by that author, but also it was treated as the same language and customs as theirs. The myths repeated in this work were also part of the heritage of these Kachinaua Indians who live on the Alto Curanja River (Schultz 1955:197–199).

An Unequal Situation

Harald Schultz traveled all over Brazil taking pictures of indigenous people who were at that time still willing to display their native dress (Schultz 1962). The Alto Purús is politically Peru, but is isolated by rain forest from the rest of Peru and since 1900 has had economic relations downriver with Brazil. So when the research expedition, which included Schultz, came up the Purús River in Brazil, they learned of the existence of various indigenous groups spread along the Curanja River. Thus, they continued on upriver. Pudicho's village was one of the two reported to be on the stream Chapuia.[9]

Schultz observed that the work load between men and women appears to be different. At first, I also thought the women worked much more than the men, but then I realized that the women put on weight and the men all stayed thin. As I went hunting with the men and helped cut gardens, I realized that they work extremely hard for various periods of time and then relax equally as diligently for a period of time.

Around 1975 we showed some of the Cashinahua men the book by Capistrano do Abreu (1914). In about fifteen minutes the younger men, who could read their language in the approved orthography, were able to decipher the orthography Capistrano used. They said it was their language, but old and a little different.

Earlier, I said that Grompes took his first wife, Maria, just before the visit by the group from San Paulo. In 1994 I was finally able to persuade Maria to speak to me—with a tape recorder running—concerning how she became his wife. Up to this time, the women had never wanted the tape recorder to hear them. The following conversation gives a little insight into the wife-husband relationship. When I requested that Grompes, the headman, tell Maria to speak to the tape recorder, he said, "I never tell Maria anything!" indicating that his role as headman did not extend that far. However, I asked Maria and she agreed. I have kept the translation quite literal in order to let most of her semantic content remain. I asked her how she came to be Grompes' wife and she replied:

> Maria: While my mother was dying with fever I was born. My father raised me and when we were coming down off the uplands I made someone to be a husband. I made an older man my husband and even though he mistreated me, I made him my husband long ago because I wanted to make someone to be a husband to me. However, I said, "In vain I am making you to be a husband. Even though you frustratingly

---

[9]Schultz's group heard the name correctly. The *ch* indicates an *sh* sound in Brazil, and the Cashinahua language uses an *x* for the *sh* sound in Peru. So *Chapuia* has the same pronunciation as *Xapu-ya* and both mean 'cotton-with'.

> try to sexually penetrate me, I am making you to be a husband. Even though I don't want to reciprocally sexually penetrate, I am making you to be a husband." Saying this I made him to be a husband long ago. Then later, being a male teenager, Grompes was liking me, a female teenager, and I made him to be a husband.
> Ricardo: Is that all? How many children?
> Maria: I have gotten [conceived] many children. I was without a male child. I got only female children. I have only one male child.
> Ricardo: Is that all?
> Maria: Yes.
> Ricardo: Where did you first live?
> Maria: At Conta I lived. Then downriver I came. After I came downriver to Balta, I was getting lots of children, when I first saw you long ago.

Maria definitely placed herself as the actor; the women are their own actors in their culturally defined roles. The wife-husband relationship is a functional arrangement. A woman needs a husband, and a man needs one or more wives; two sisters seems to work best. Maria was a co-wife with her sister Ana, running a household for a very good hunter, who at times was able to attract other women to join his household. Maria and Ana are considered successful because they have grown children to care for them in their old age, especially daughters.

Pudicho continues his story by telling how they came to live at Conta, mentioned above by Maria.

> 54. From there I came further downstream long ago. While I was coming downstream the Yaminahuas said to me, "Here at Conta [on the Curanja] make a garden." So I started clearing the land; after I cut the plot, I burned it and did the planting. After I built a house with many helpers, I settled there eating from that garden. Then the outsider [Dini Fulano] again had me collect rubber. I thought out loud, "I intend to collect rubber again," and went downriver for a few months. After I had gone downriver for a few months, I went upriver for a few months.

The caucho tree, *Castilloa elastica*, does not yield sap by being scarred as the *seringue* tree, *Hevea brasiliensis*, which is most often considered as the rubber tree. The caucho tree has to be cut down and the bark slashed at the crotches to drain the sap. These trees grow at a slightly higher altitude

An Unequal Situation

than the *seringue* trees and are a renewable resource because they grow back rather quickly. Because, like most trees in the rain forest, they are found scattered among the other species, Pudicho had to go a long way from the village to find them. He usually went with a group of men. They would set up a camp and then search out all the caucho trees on each streamlet of the side streams that flow into the main river. Sometimes they planned a year in advance and cut a small garden plot for cassava and plantains to eat, along with the animals they shot while hunting for the caucho trees. Sometimes the wives and youngest children would go along to keep camp. Once the trees were cut down and the bark slashed, it took several days for the latex to drain into the holes they dug below each slash. The congealed latex balls were then brought back to the village and combined into approximately 50-kilo balls for shipping. They did not have to smoke the latex, as was done with the *seringue* latex. The caucho latex was still being collected and sold in the early 1970s.

7

Different Outsiders

At this point Pudicho's group decided to stay on the Curanja River and work for the river traders. Dini Fulano was the Cashinahua's principal connection with the outside world, but they knew that there were other outsiders living in and around Puerto Esperanza, farther downriver on the Purus River. Puerto Esperanza, being the only official town in the district, had a Civil Guard detachment which carried on most governmental functions. The location was chosen because it had level ground for an air strip which did not flood even in the heaviest rainy seasons. At that time the officials were heavily influenced by mercantile interests, that paid the indigenous people little for what they produced and charged them artificially high prices for what they purchased. The river traders, including Dini Fulano, spoke openly of "owning" their indebted indigenous clients. The Civil Guard regarded all the indigenous people as minors without legal standing. This attitude had some basis in law because at that time an indebted person could not move or change his line of work without the permission of the owner of his debt. However, Fulano was not giving each client a written account of his debts as required by law and thus had no legal basis for his proprietary attitude. He functioned only by a gentlemen's agreement with the other river traders—that the trader who first brought a group into a contact situation had first call on their labor (Hemming 1987:253).

This was the prevailing situation when the Summer Institute of Linguistics (SIL) began to send linguistic investigators to the Purús River area of Peru to study the then unwritten indigenous languages. It was their goal to do linguistic studies, produce phonetic orthographies, and then aid the Ministry of Education in establishing bilingual schools in each village which would use the approved orthographies. The government also gave SIL permission to fulfill their further goal of translating the Bible into the indigenous languages. In 1955 the first SIL linguists to contact Pudicho's group were Kenneth Kensinger and Eugene Scott. Scott later transferred to working with the Sharanahua and Marinahua, two of the groups the Cashinahua call Yaminahua. Pudicho tells of their coming as follows.

> 55. At about that time I was told that when others of our people first came into existence long ago, our parent god had created them long ago. Then there was a different man, who was not a real Peruvian; he was a different one of our people. Real outsiders are Peruvians. This different one wrote a letter about me [to the authorities downriver] saying, "I want to learn their words. Write to them for me; because if you send a letter for me, they will do it."
>
> Then a Peruvian delivered a letter to me. After I heard about the message, I quit collecting rubber and came back to live in Conta long ago. While I was there, some Yaminahuas brought these others upriver for me; there were two of this different type of our people.

As the Yaminahua were bringing them upriver, they met Fulano and some Cashinahua men. Pudicho's sister's son Mario told me about this first meeting.

> Okay, friend, how I grew up and then how you met us long ago, I am telling. However, you were not first; Roberto and Ken met us first long ago. I am again telling you, listen. How I lived as time passed, how I studied, the manner in which my thinking went, how my thinking grew, I am telling you.
>
> At first Ken and Roberto met us. When they encountered us, I was with a village leader. That is true, not a lie. I was there. I was following a village leader all around in order to learn whatever we were doing; whatever good that he was doing, he was teaching me. While working for an outsider, we were continually causing him to look approvingly on us. The village leader made me follow him and learn from him as we came downriver to collect turtle eggs.
>
> At about that time, Cecilio, the first of your people to come to the Yaminahua, was teaching them and asked, "Do some other type of Genuine people live upriver?"
>
> "Cashinahua Genuine people live there," they reported to him, so I was told.

Cecilio then told his people about us, I was told, your people that is. Then Ken and Roberto heard the news about us. And then, so that they could be with us, and cause us to learn reading and writing, and cause us to learn that the outsiders were cheating us, and that we were losing our traditional way of life, their leader sent them and they came here long ago.

Even though we did not know about it, they came in an airplane and it descended to the earth downriver from here. While they continued to think of us, the Yaminahua were bringing them upriver. At the same time we were coming downriver from Conta in order to eat turtle eggs, and we met them. We were with our leader Grompes; I and Grompes and brother Adolfo and another, Tufi, that number of us were coming downriver thinking of eating turtle eggs and at a side stream named Pedro, we met them. A cold front was making us very cold when we met them as they were coming with the Yaminahua. The Yaminahua Alfonso, Pablo, and Vesantillo were taking them upriver when we met them.

After we met them, the Yaminahua said to us, "Good. Our friends came from their very distant community the other day. It is reported to them that the outsiders always cheat us. So they came thinking of us and first landed at our village. They are presently teaching us. From there also they sent these two and they also came down in an airplane at our village. I have been causing them to think of you while bringing them upriver for you. What do you think of the idea? Give it some thought, also!"

We responded, "Good, we would like it if the outsiders were not able to cheat us."

Then one of the Yaminahuas said, "They are coming so that the outsiders may not cheat you again. When you collect rubber, they always cheat you. And when you get skins, they always cheat you. Wanting to cause you all to learn how they cheat you, they came the other day. After they arrived, I said to them, 'I'll take you upriver.' And they said, 'Good.' That's how it was the other day."

Then we said, "Good. We go along with that. We are happy. How goes it with Ken and Roberto?—I mean Scotty—What do they have to say?"

Then Alfonso said to them for us, "They say that they like you all very much."

Ken said, "Very good," and being happy he gave one of his flashlights to each one of us individually. I took one from him. Scotty gave another one to my leader in order to make us friendly. The one Ken gave me was good.

Then Dini, the one who said, "Go to get turtle eggs for me," and brought us downriver yesterday, was angry toward us because we were talking with Ken and Scotty and said in our words, "Don't speak with them! Don't make talk with them; they might sexually penetrate your wives. They might tie up your wives to your detriment and sexually penetrate them for sure! Don't take those ones upriver!"

We did not listen to him. We went and spoke with them anyway. Being resentful towards us, Dini went a good distance away and hung his hammock separately to sleep. We spoke with them long into the night. "How is it?" we asked.

Then Ken said, "I have come to live temporarily with you all. Wanting to cause you to learn, wanting to cause you to write words, I came today. While learning your words, I want to cause you to learn the outsiders' words also. I intend also to see how the outsiders always cheat you and how you have lived. To do all that I came today."

We said, "Good," and fell asleep at their campsite.

After sleeping, we awoke and went upriver with them. At that time we did not yet have a motor so we poled along upriver. While it was very cold, we poled along and then poled along some more and again slept. Then going from there we entered our village of Conta. After we entered Conta, Dini said to our leader, "Don't talk with them anymore, all of you."

Ken and Scotty were acting timidly and did not understand his words. Then we reported to our people saying, "Our outsider boss always cheats us a lot. The outsiders always steal from us."

Then Ken said, "I myself am not like that. Intending to live with you and teach you, we came today." We were happy to hear this.

Then our boss Dini said to them, "There, somewhere far away upriver I encountered them years ago and have always made them work. Don't try to take ownership. Don't talk with them!" However, even though he spoke strongly, Dini was continually timid towards them.

Different Outsiders 81

I have left what Mario told me in 1994 uncorrected. Mario forgot that Eugene Scott, known as "Scotty", came on that first trip, and realized his mistake part way through his story. Another discrepancy is that Ken Kensinger says Mario was not present at that meeting. He remembers only Adolfo and Tufi being with Fulano. Kensinger says also that Mario put many words into his mouth to support his memory and that he did not yet know even one word in their language. The Yaminahua may have interjected the purpose of combating the cheating by the outsiders as they translated what Kensinger said in Spanish. They were probably projecting their own hopes onto the visit of these outsiders. Although not all of the outsider traders mistreated the Cashinahua, cheating is an ongoing theme to this day. Kensinger remembers Dini Fulano's reaction to their coming much as Mario related it, which clearly illustrates Fulano's proprietary attitude.

Pudicho continues his account of Ken and Scotty's arrival as follows.

56. The Yaminahua brought me only two; one of them [Ken] said to me, "Are you not going to kill me? While I am making you my friend, don't kill me! I am afraid that when I have fallen asleep, you might kill us. Someone might club us or shoot us in our sleep. Don't kill us."

Then I replied, "I will not shoot you. Where would I want to live, and what would I be doing, if I intended to shoot you? I will live with you. I never shoot Peruvians. I never shoot Brazilians. I never shoot Yaminahuas. I am a good man. After I have lived with you, I want very much to work for you."

57. Then he said, "I will live here with you for the time being to learn your words. Over there in the Ucayali Valley, my people are learning the words of the various groups. I asked about this side [Purús] and was told about you, the Genuine people. I was told that it is said that the Genuine people are good people. So, when I heard that, I came and made contact with you today. Make a house for me, so I can also visit and continually live with you," he was saying.

At that time Kensinger and Scott were communicating through the Yaminahua, so that some of the concepts expressed in this conversation may have become clear to Pudicho only over a period of a few years.

Mario, Pudicho's nephew, has some additional details concerning this first visit.

> Not listening at all to Dini, we made them feel welcome; we made Scotty and Ken accustomed to us. After we made them feel welcome, they had us build a house for them. Because they were without a house, they were saying, "Make a house for us. Make a house for me. I came yesterday to cause you to learn. I came wanting to observe you. Make me a house."
>
> Then the village leader made us build a house; we built a large house for them, and they paid us for our work—they gave us beads without being stingy; they gave us soap; they gave us mosquito nets; they gave us clothes. Then being very happy, we worked hard and quickly brought the two sides of the roof together at the top of their large house.
>
> After their house was closed up for them, they settled into it. In order to learn a few words they were asking us about everything, and were learning small words, not large ones. That's how we all lived there.

Pudicho continues his account of the same initial visit with a little overlap.

> 58. Then my son [Grompes] had our men build a house for them and they paid them with machetes, blankets, mosquito nets, and axes. Then he [Ken] said to me, "Don't work for the outsiders any more; I myself, I am making you mine. Continue to stay here at this same place. Live here as a Genuine man. Don't again be as outsiders. Outsiders are ones who maltreat others. If you give them your garden produce you won't have anything to eat. By eating up your garden produce on you, the outsiders are taking advantage of you. Stay and live at this place." After he said this to me, he gave my people things as he was leaving; he started going and coming long ago, taking my brother first.

After the Yaminahua, who brought them upriver, went back downriver, Ken and Scotty were on their own. Pudicho may have remembered Ken's language-learning ability as being quicker than it in fact was. Some of the above dialogue may have taken place during his second visit in 1956. In an article written years later, Kensinger tells of his early language-learning experiences.

> The problem of communication is greatly increased when the factors of totally different cultures and totally different languages are added to the equation. Just how difficult the

problem is under such circumstances became painfully obvious to me during my fieldwork with the Cashinahua. When I first arrived in one of their villages I did not speak or understand a single word of their language, nor did they speak or understand any language I could use, and no interpreters were available.

I began to learn Cashinahua by pointing at an object and asking, in English, Spanish, or Portuguese (the latter two being the trade languages of the area), what it was and trying to write down what was said. The responses were disappointing and confusing because they all seemed to sound similar, having a common base, *men*, with other syllables attached. Obviously, they did not understand me and I did not understand them. Some days later I learned that in Cashinahua one does not point with one's finger, one points with one's lip, which is just as accurate as with the finger once one learns to follow an imaginary line from the curve of the lip to the object. Among the Cashinahua the only time one points with a finger is when making a legal accusation, a very serious matter. The words spoken in response to my question had been 'It is his finger', 'his hand', 'He is pointing', etc., all of which contained the morpheme *men* meaning 'hand'. Once I learned the question, *Hawamen*, 'What is it?' (the *men* in this utterance means 'question' not 'hand'), I was able to collect the names of all kinds of objects, but I was not able to converse with anyone because to do so I needed verbs; one cannot point at verbs, either with one's finger or one's lip. More about eliciting verb forms later.

In collecting the names of objects, I became aware of sound contrasts like the initial sounds in *paka*, 'bamboo', *baka*, 'fish', *taka*, 'liver', *daka*, 'to rest', *kakan*, 'basket', etc. Many of the sounds used in Cashinahua are similar to those in English as in the words above. However, in Cashinahua as in all languages, what appear to us to be slight differences in sound often produce striking differences in meaning, as when I referred to a woman using the term *shanu* which I thought meant 'grandmother' or 'old woman'. She responded with anger because I had inadvertently called her a rattlesnake (an insulting term sometimes used to refer to women who gossip). The correct term is very similar to *shanu*, however, the initial 'sh' sound is made with the tip of the tongue turned back resulting in *xanu*, which does mean 'grandmother'....

Verbs were easier to elicit once I had learned the meaning and proper usage of *min hawa wai*. I had guessed that the form meant 'What are you doing?' However, when I responded to that form with a statement of what I was doing, the questioners seemed to be insulted. When I asked a man who was sitting in his hammock, sharpening his arrow, *min hawa wai*, he responded *en hawamaki*, the same response I got from his wife who was grinding corn, and from his young daughter who was playing. Several days later, I sat in my hammock watching two children playing a game of chase. One of them ran into the side of a large clay pot full of about five gallons of corn gruel. It cracked and spilled its contents on the ground. The child's mother called out to the child, *min hawa wai*. The response was *en hawamaki*. The mother repeated her question, *min hawa wai*. The child answered, *en beyusai* 'I'm playing'. (I knew this form). As I puzzled over this verbal exchange, I did not know what it all meant, but I guessed that my original hunch that *min hawa wai* meant 'What are you doing?' was correct. A little later one of the men came into the house and said, *min hawa wai*, to which I replied *en hawamaki*. He repeated his question, *min hawa wai*. I replied, *en disin dakai*, 'I'm resting in the hammock'. He whooped and laughed, running from the house only to return with his brother. The sequence was repeated: *min hawa wai*. - *en hawamaki* - *min hawa wai* - *en disin dakai*. His response was the same as his brother's had been. And more men were called to repeat the sequence. I was mystified, but they were happy. I had learned something important. But what?

Some time later, I realized what it all meant. *Min hawa wai* does mean 'what are you doing?' and *en hawamaki* means 'I'm not doing anything.' However, the significance does not lie in the meaning of the words but in the sequence and the cultural rules. The question is not asked in order to find out what a person is doing. One's actions are visible. Rather it is a query about one's mood. If the response to the initial question is a statement of one's activity, the implication is that the individual is busy and does not wish to be bothered, or that he is not in the mood to be sociable. A response of *en hawamaki* 'I'm not doing anything', implies 'Pull up a turtle shell and talk.' (Kensinger 1975:13–17)

Different Outsiders

We appreciate everything Ken and Scotty went through in their language learning because, even though much of the basic linguistics was done and an orthography established, we also had to learn this entirely different pattern of thinking when we arrived fourteen years later. More about those frustrations later, but now Pudicho tells how Kensinger investigated their language and culture.

> 59. After he took my brother Belisario to the other side [Pucallpa] by airplane, he was the first one he asked about our words long ago; asking for words, he asked about our speech. Belisario sang songs for him; he told him how we used to work, how we always shoot game animals and all about how we used to live long ago. After Belisario did that, he [Ken] came back, and took me also long ago.
>
> 60. He took me to the other side [Pucallpa] by airplane; he took me by airplane intending to bring me back. So that I would teach him my words, he was asking me how I used to live long ago, how I used to kill animals, how I used to work, how I came to have a wife, how I started sexually penetrating women, and how I started having children. By asking questions, he finished getting my words.
>
> 61. After he brought me back to Conta, he said to the men, "Make an airplane landing strip. So that airplanes can come down here, make an airplane field. It is bad when I descend onto the river." After they heard this, the men tried to make an airplane field, but rejected it as not possible.
>
> 62. After they tried to make a landing strip and rejected it, my Genuine men, who constantly want things, were drooling and variously saying out loud, "In order to get lots of things, I am moving away. I am going to get a mosquito net. I am going to get a gun. I am going to get a large pot." By saying these things, they alarmed him and his friend [Ken Kensinger and Robert Cromack]. Thinking that they were all going to leave for Brazil, they said to them, "Don't do it." Because my people were talking of leaving, they said to them, "Don't do it! Don't do it!"

Even though Ken Kensinger and Robert Cromack, who had replaced Scotty, were more fluent in their language ability, they were learning some of the reasons behind the Cashinahua men's friendship with them. The Cashinahua men had not forgotten their original reason for making contact on the Peru side of the border. Pudicho's brother, Idiodoro, has more to say about their relationship with the traders who came to extend credit and thereby draw them into debt-peonage. Idiodoro says:

> While we were living in this condition, Dini mistreated us by giving us cheap shirts and pants without pockets and bad mosquito nets without sleeves for hammock strings, thus we could not use them with hammocks. And by means of the tremendous amount of rubber that we collected for him only Dini got new false teeth; we didn't get any teeth, only he got new teeth. When he left to go get his new teeth he was throwing us away, not providing work for us. He said, "I am going over to the other side to live," then he left and we learned that he got his new teeth. Then when he came back for a visit, we had learned a few more Spanish words and said to him, "You continually mistreated us long ago. When we were young teenagers who knew only a few Spanish words, you repeatedly mistreated us long ago. You mistreated our people long ago."
>
> But he said, "It was nothing. I did not know the correct way of living when I did it to them long ago. Don't say that about me anymore!" I did not hear him say this, someone told me. But at this time I always hear about how he is living over on the other side [in Pucallpa].
>
> However, back then other river traders came; after Dini had gone, Gamboa came. However, we saw Herman Torres first; he is the one who started making us work after Dini left. I did not work for him, others did. I worked only for Dini and Gamboa. I also worked for Cabo Díaz; he was very good. He lived in Esperanza long ago, but he has now left. We went there from Conta to see him and he told us to work, saying, "Do rubber," and gave us shotguns long ago. He also gave me a shotgun. He did well; he paid well and gave us metal pots and various other things in trade for rubber. However, when Gamboa contacted us we left our work with Cabo Díaz. When Gamboa first came, we also collected rubber for him. Then when they stopped taking rubber, we hunted for skins.
>
> When Cabo Díaz was helping us, we were living in Conta, and it was there that Ken first contacted us. He contacted my brother Pudicho first. It was from there I went to Brazil to live. Then after my other brother Belisario had taken

possession of this village Balta, he went and brought me back here; now I live here.

When Gamboa was working with us, he ordered us to hunt skins, and we followed his words. We took cat skins, peccary skins, nutria skins, and all types of skins, especially jaguar and ocelot skins. As Gamboa took these skins, he gave my people motors. He also gave them metal pots and other things, but at that time my people knew only a little about things. However, they got guns, axes, machetes, knives, and sewing machines.

Idiodoro has given a rough outline of the river traders who followed Dini Fulano. I knew all these traders and a few more who were still functioning when we arrived in 1969. Cabo Díaz is Corporal Díaz of the Civil Guard, who told me that he was in the first airplane to fly members of the Civil Guard out to the Purús to occupy that territory. This was to prevent Brazilian peasants from filtering in and taking the area away from Peru as they had taken all of what is now western Brazil. Previously, the Civil Guard had to go upriver on tributaries of the Ucayali River and walk across the high jungle. Then they carved out temporary canoes from palm trees to go down to the frontier to maintain the headwaters of both the Purús and Juruá rivers as Peruvian territory. Díaz had married a daughter of one of the backwoods families and was content to spend the rest of his civil service career on the Purús River. He was kind to the indigenous people in his own way. He was the one who told me directly that they were all legally minors and were under the care of the state. Several orphans from various indigenous groups grew up in his household as house-boys and general helpers. He saw to it that they learned to speak Spanish, eat their meals in a "civilized" manner with salt, and go to school as much as possible. Joaquín, one of the Cashinahua men, tells of his early desire to gain the outsiders' ways and things and of the resistance to this by his sister's husband, Pudicho's brother Belisario.

Good, my name is Joaquín Cumapa Jiménez, when I speak listen to me. I am going to tell you about how my parent abandoned me when I was a little child; listen to me.

When I wasn't grown yet and still small, when my teeth were starting to change, my female parent abandoned me. From then on my male parent was raising me and I was growing. When I was at the age of starting to hunt, my male parent crossed over to the Embira River and also abandoned me long ago, I am telling you. After he had been gone for months and we did not see him, we knew that my male parent had abandoned us. And there I was, my brother-in-law and my sister were feeding me and raising me. He had me go with him all the time and showed me his work and how to shoot.

Then as I was growing I was thinking, "Has my thinking come to me? I am learning to think." While observing his work, I myself was also thinking, "I am going to go to the outsiders. I want to learn the outsiders' words. I am suffering without clothes." While continuing to think this, I went to Corporal Díaz; I went to live under the authority of the Civil Guard Corporal Díaz. After I arrived, Corporal Díaz took charge of me and was feeding me when he said, "Okay, you are a little child, you don't do heavy work. Only fetch water for the house and bring in the firewood that the others split." So I settled there and was working for him when he sent me to school with his children. I did not attend for a year, only one month. Then my brother-in-law came to Esperanza; Ken was taking him to the other side [Pucallpa]. My brother-in-law said to me, "It shouldn't be this way. I have left your niece and sister alone by coming away. Go and fish for food for your niece!" Thus, he sent me back.

I came back with those who brought him downriver; I came to Conta, which is very far upriver. My sister was settled there, thinking of me as if I were a little child. But I was not lazy. I cut firewood for her; I fished for her; I built a blind near some fallen fruit and shot *yutillos* and doves for her. I was settled in and feeding my niece who has since died.

Then my brother-in-law, who had gone with Ken to Yarina, came back, met me and said, "How goes it?"

I replied, "I am settled in. Since you sent me back, I have provided my small take to my niece and sister to eat." It was when he started flying in the airplane that I settled there upriver. Next I thought, "Am I a grown man?" I was a grown man, brave and prepared. So I again went to be among the outsiders; I was following my own thinking; no one was sending me. And even though my brother-in-law tried to hold me back, I would not listen, and I went to be among the outsiders.

While I was becoming accustomed to them, some outsiders wanted to take me to Pucallpa and said to me, "Good, I am taking you to make you be my child."

However, some Yaminahuas heard this and went to my brother-in-law who was at the mouth of the Curanja and said, "What do you want to do by making your wife's brother into an outsider? Their people don't live with us. Bring him here. Don't send your wife's brother with the outsiders." Many were saying the same thing.

He thought and then went downriver to Esperanza and scolded me, saying, "Not this! Go see your older sister for a while! Your older sister is thinking of you; take care of her! Don't live separate from them and take on outsider customs."

I replied, "Okay, I will listen to your word. Only you are my other parent; another man would not be that way to me. I will listen to your words." He then took me to Conta; to the same Conta I had left months before. He took me and I settled in; working with him, I settled in.

Then another cross-cousin, my uncle Araguana's son, my older cross-cousin, who later died, he was thinking other thoughts and came saying, "Let's all go and live downriver. Let's go and live on the Purús." Agreeing to this we were coming downriver. But the Yaminahua did not want us to go too far because they had laid claim to the area downriver. So we arrived at the side stream Balta and Belisario said, "This is not what we planned, but let's stay at this place," and he made us stay there. Even though some resisted, he finally made us stay and we made a temporary shelter and settled in. Then we started cutting the underbrush to make a garden; he was making me work continually. I was working with him and after we cut all the underbrush, we felled the trees. Those of us in the first group were me, my cousin Mario, my uncle Araguana, my older brother, and my other cousin Leoncio; we came and made a garden long ago.

Joaquín gives us an insight into the desires and conflicts that were, I suspect, in the minds of many of the indigenous people at that time, not just the Cashinahua. Pudicho's story continues at the time of the move from Conta downriver to Balta with a slightly different viewpoint.

63. Later Belisario said, "Here at Conta, it is bad. When the river floods, the banks always collapse. Let's change our place. Let's move our village to a different side stream." Thinking this, my brother came here and made a garden long ago. After many months when his garden was complete and

he had built a house, I came downriver and joined him.
While enlarging his garden for him, I also built a house.

Again, Joaquín has more to say about that move to Balta and how he was not yet settled in his mind to remain there. He also identifies Pudicho's son Grompes as their leader. As we saw earlier, Dini Fulano had put it into Grompes' mind to be the leader, literally 'place parent'; but I know that Pudicho had not yet retired from leadership at that time. So there must have been a time when the leadership of the son increased as that of the father decreased. Leadership among the Cashinahua is not overtly obvious, as I found out later. Joaquín continues his account.

> Then later our leader, my older brother Grompes, also came. After he came with his people, he also was making a garden and said to us, "We don't have anything to eat. Go get bananas." We went to an old Chaninahua garden and got a few bananas as we continued to work. We burned the dried garden area and planted corn. Then while I was planting manioc, everyone was hungry and after a few months began to eat that which had sprouted. While we were there Ken also came again.
>
> Ken had been looking for us; he came down in his airplane at Conta and I was told that various ones said, "Your people are not here! Far downriver at Balta they went months ago." Thus, they came in their airplane looking and when they saw us, they put down on the river. We then made a house for him.
>
> Several months after we had built a house for him and he had settled in, he brought many of his people to visit. He brought John, Roberto, and others with various names. He [Ken] settled in and worked with them. John collected bird skins and various animal skins; he also made me work for him. He said, "Hunt for me," and I hunted for him.

During the rainy season the Curanja River has enough water for a small airplane with floats to put down on it. Also, there is a straight stretch of river at Balta long enough for take-offs, but there are often sunken logs which make its use dangerous unless someone walks and wades most of its length to assure that it is safe. So it was used only at high-water times or in cases of emergency. The friends Kensinger brought to visit in Balta were graduate students from Louisiana State University doing doctoral research. Three of them returned for a visit in 1971, bringing John McIlhenny, who had aided them financially in their research in that very remote area of Amazonia. John O'Neal is an ornithologist; Richard Gardener is a mammalogist; and the other (whose name I have forgotten) is a herpetologist. Joaquín continues.

> Then I again separated myself in order to work for the outsiders. I was thinking, "I am now a grown man. Being a grown man, I am going to go and work with the outsiders." I went and walked with the outsiders, accommodating myself to the way they do things. An outsider was watching me and said, "Okay, let's work. Don't go to your people again; I will make you work." He made me work continually. At that time I had not yet been made to take a wife.
>
> Then in order to make it so I could no longer imitate the outsiders, Maditoba's people arranged for me to have a wife. At first, she rejected me but she then made me feel at peace with them; I was continually coming to be at peace with them and settled in. Working for them, I settled in with them months and months ago.
>
> Friend, That's all; it's good.

Joaquín still had the desire to be with the outsiders and obtain outsider goods. This continues to be true, but he gave me a clear statement of what marriage means to a young Cashinahua man. Young men are drawn into a household, sometimes by the daughter, but usually by the mother and father, who acquire the benefit of his labor. As was illustrated by Pudicho's parents many years before, the daughter often rejects the husband at first but slowly accepts the arrangement because her mother wants it. The Cashinahua practice trial marriage even though they do not think of it in that way. The in-marrying young man has to prove himself to his wife, her father, and especially to her mother, or he finds himself rejected. If they reject him, he is divorced unless the wife chooses to leave her parents and go with him. Marriage is primarily a functional arrangement. If the man and woman fulfill their cultural roles well, it is considered a good marriage. As daughters do not ordinarily leave their mothers, bride service continues for the husband as long as his wife's parents live. The women are very careful to instill this idea in their daughters so that they will be provided for in their old age.

By the time Pudicho's group moved to Balta, the Cashinahua men were losing their fear of associating with the outsider Peruvians and were learning some of their technology. Belisario tells us his feelings about that transition period.

While I was living like that, my brother was the leader of our group and made contact with the outsiders for me. He did this even though I was afraid because I had never seen them. I had always heard the Ancient Ones' stories about them, so I was afraid of them. I had not seen the outsiders yet and I incorrectly thought, "They are like peccary or some other game animal." After that they came to our village to see us and when I saw them, I was in awe, thinking, "Are they really like that with somewhat long hair?" I then rejected them because of their hair. But now my hair is the same way. I am now also an outsider; my hair is somewhat long also; I buy their manufactured things; I go on living as one who continually obtains outsider things.

We used to live in the upland areas long ago without canoes. But when I saw the outsiders making canoes I was learning by thinking in my head and in the same way I saw them do it, I made a canoe and always travel by that means now. And when it came to making their type of house, I told myself, "Watch what they are doing." Then I watched those who made houses and whatever they did I took notice of and learned. Now when I make a house to live in, I make a house like theirs. When I went downriver long ago, to where the outsiders lived, I saw their things, all kinds of things, and now I use the same things as I continue to live my life.

When I did not yet live here in Balta I lived way upriver at the mouth of the Xapuya. It was up at its headwaters that my father engendered me. It was at the mouth of the Xapuya that my older brother made contact with the outsiders for me. It was from there that I moved downriver in stages, living at the mouth of each side stream and then I finally lived here at Balta. Listen well to what I told you today!

Before an airstrip was built in Balta, the linguists Kensinger and Cromack usually went downriver by canoe to the mouth of the Curanja. There they met an airplane to take them and their language assistants to Yarinacocha, where the jungle center of SIL was located. After they took the older men, Belisario and Pudicho, they took younger men like Pudicho's son Grompes, and eventually Mario, Pudicho's sister's son, who later became the first school teacher. Mario tells how he started on that long, difficult road.

After we had lived there for a while, my leader Grompes said to me, "Okay, what we agreed months ago is approaching. Can you go? 'Tell him for me,' Ken told me today. I am asking you because of what he said. Listen to him."

Later Ken said to me, "Can you go?"

I responded, "I can go."

Then he said, "Are you not afraid?"

I said, "I am not afraid."

Then he asked, "When you miss your wife, can you avoid touching another woman?"

I answered, "When I am lonely, I am able to not touch."

Again he asked, "When you miss your wife and your parents, are you able to avoid weeping?"

I answered, "I am able to not weep. My heart is strong."

Then he said, "Good. I shall take you." Then as another moon was finishing Ken said, "Go. Let's go together," and we started downriver by canoe to meet the airplane. As I was going downriver I did not understand airplanes; I did not know what it meant to go by means of an airplane. Thinking mistakenly that everything was okay, I was very happy. In that condition he took me downriver and we arrived at the mouth of the Curanja River where the Marinahua and the Sharanahua were living. It was from there that they talked to the airplane [radio communication with the pilot].

After they called the airplane, a large Cessna airplane came and descended to the ground. The pilot said to us, "Did you come today? How many passengers are there?"

Concerning us, Ken said, "This amount came today."

Then the pilot said, "Good. Let's go," and he loaded us into the airplane. After he had loaded us along with my leader Grompes, he took us away. Not being used to an airplane yet, I sat hunched over, being afraid to look. The airplane caused me to feel nauseous as we went along; feeling nauseous, I wanted to vomit. Finally, he brought me down to the ground over there at Yarinacocha. After he brought me down the pilot looked at me; I was okay and I was not homesick.

Then I think it was Ken who said, "Okay, my friend has gotten a place for us to live." He was speaking about his leader Eugene, the linguist with the Kapanahua. Going to Eugene's place, we lived in his storehouse, the place Ken had gotten for us months before. We lived with our friend Ken.

It was there that Roberto first taught me; he instructed me a little bit in writing and arithmetic. He did not do a lot of teaching; he taught me during the daytime only. However, by myself I kept studying at night, thinking, "Is this how the outsiders always do it?" Thinking that, I was learning sums and multiplication.

And because I was doing that, Roberto wrote for me in Genuine words. By writing for me, Ken and Roberto first caused me to learn writing. *Atsa pive* ['Cassava eat'], *ka* ['go'], *kape* ['caimán'], *Kebu bake taka pive* ['Turkey-like bird's offspring's liver eat'], they wrote; at first they caused me to learn that amount. When I had learned those, Roberto said, "Wow, he knows a lot. This youngster knows a lot. Where did you learn? Did you go to school?"

I answered, "I have not gone to school. However, when a trader was cheating us by detrimentally taking our work, our things, our rubber, our animal skins, and whatever else we had, he did his sums and threw the paper away. I picked it up and had been studying it when my boss's son, with whom I collected rubber, began teaching me as he was doing his sums and making out his accounts, saying, "Someone can do it this way." Because he was teaching me and transferred to me a small amount of knowledge, I am in the process of learning."

"Good. Your head is very good," they said, but were wondering about it and secretly observed me long ago, giving attention to my thinking, that is. However, Roberto was also wondering, "Hmm, he could be a good teacher. We can make this one into a teacher. This teenager is very good," he thought and kept me under observation.

While he was watching and teaching me, one of your people's teenagers [Victor Loos] came to me and said, "Mario, do you know arithmetic, as they are saying?" Then he did long multiplication for me and I was learning it. He said, "Very good!" and was causing me to learn more as the days passed, but they prohibited him, saying, "Don't teach him. He himself can do it. We can make him into a teacher."

I did not understand their words as they were speaking, but I myself kept learning. Then after they had kept us there for six months, Ken said to me, "Okay, are you not missing your wife?"

I answered, "I am not homesick."

However, he said, "Let's go back temporarily," and brought us back here long ago. Bringing me, they brought me down to the ground; I descended to Balta by means of an airplane.

Different Outsiders

> After I came down, I thought over their ideas about my being a teacher and settled back into regular life.

Pudicho now continues his story, telling how the airstrip at Balta came to be built, something which has had long-term political consequences.

> 64. Then the other man [Robert] said to us, "So that I can come directly here in an airplane and live with you, make an airplane field. So that I can give you medicines when you suffer pain, so that I can bring cloth for you, so that I can bring shotgun shells for you, make an airplane landing field." This is how he had us build an airplane field. We made a good landing field; then a pilot brought an airplane down on it.
>
> 65. While we were living by the landing strip, he taught another child of mine to learn the outsiders' writing. It was while he was teaching him to read and write that the one who first contacted me, the other boss, made me fly in an airplane; he took me also to the other side [Pucallpa] and had me tell him many words. By continually repeating my words, he finished getting my words after several months and then returning, we came back long ago.

Pudicho reports that Robert Cromack justifies turning their gardens into an airstrip by saying it would expedite their getting the things most important to them at that time: (1) shotgun shells so the men could more easily get meat which everyone craved, (2) cloth to replace body painting so the women could be beautiful and stop being eyed by the river traders, and (3) medicines for the many ailments that their leaf medicines could not cure. The other child that Pudicho says Cromack was teaching was actually his nephew Mario, his sister's son. Mario has much more to say about his struggle to become a teacher. But first Mario tells more about his trips to Yarinacocha.

> Then they again took me; they took me and my maternal uncle Belisario. After we arrived, I read words out loud; Roberto caused me to read words out loud. While he was having me read and learn many things, he wondered if my words were clear enough. Then at the same time he was having us labor for him; Roberto was building a house and asked us to work. So we dug dirt for him; we finished all the digging for the house. Then in preparation for us to come home, he got us a lot of things. He got shot guns for us; he got a guitar for me; and he gave us lots of clothes. Everything was

good and after we had come back here for a few months, he again took us. He liked me because I was learning to read and write and again took me to Yarinacocha. Over there I was learning well and I was not afraid of the outsiders. And as he was listening to me speaking the outsiders' words, Roberto wondered, "Okay, I guess we can make a teacher out of him."

At that time I was not thinking of becoming a teacher. When I saw them studying, those who were teachers before me, the Aguaruna, the Piro, and those of various other groups, I thought, "Why are they doing that? They say they are studying." However, I was misinterpreting what they were doing. Then Roberto asked me, "Can you go to class and study?"

I said, "I can study."

So he said, "Good. Wait for the time being." That was all he said. I was thinking that he may have been mistaken when he said that to me. I continued to think of this after we came back here and while I was repeatedly working with him. Later Ken called only me to come to Yarinacocha. After I went there, John, along with Ken, made an agreement with me, saying, "Okay, can I take you to the United States?"

I responded, "Yes, I can go with you."

John again said, "You are a very good man. I can show you some very large cities."

Then Ken said, "Good, you can go and see them. I shall send you a message when it is time to go."

But because Ken and his friends took blood samples in Balta, Raúl did something bad long ago. Doing bad, Raúl Díaz made a denunciation against Ken. After we had signed the denunciation against him, Ken was not able to come again; only Roberto remained.

While John O'Neil was doing research for his Ph.D. he learned enough Cashinahua language to carry on daily life and, as Joaquín indicated, he could tell the hunters the types of birds he was looking for. The taking of blood samples and extensive body measurements was done by a group of physical anthropologists from the University of Pennsylvania, where Kensinger had started graduate studies in anthropology during his furlough times. They had permission from the authorities in Lima, and had checked with the officials in the provincial capital Pucallpa. But they had failed to pass through Puerto Esperanza to notify officials there of their scientific project and official permission. In Peru, each governmental level is jealous of its prerogatives and authority, even though all major decisions are executed from the top down. Raúl Díaz is a Cashinahua who grew up in Corporal Díaz's household as an orphan. He probably reported the taking of blood samples to Díaz, who at that time was the ruling official in Puerto Esperanza. Because he viewed all indigenous people as legal minors under his protection, he sent for the leading men of Balta to come to Puerto Esperanza. Some of them told me that they were verbally forced to put their thumb prints on the document without understanding the contents even though Corporal Díaz told them in Spanish. This occurred after the scientific team had left and was instrumental in Kensinger's not being able to continue his work with the Cashinahua.

After Kensinger left, Cromack continued his efforts to help Mario become a paid bilingual school teacher and then establish an official school in Balta. Mario continues:

> Then Roberto said to me, "Okay, I see that you are very good; you can teach. You can teach them in your village. Are you able to be a teacher?"
>
> I said, "I don't know. I can do it. I can teach them." I was mistakenly thinking that it was good to say, "I can be that. I can do it."
>
> Then Roberto said, "Good. I can make you a teacher. I told my leaders about you and they said, 'Good' to me the other day. I can help you."
>
> I responded, "Very good. I can be a teacher."
>
> Then he said, "Enter the course," and I started the Bilingual School Teacher Training Course. After I started, someone stole my storage box with all the eating utensils Roberto had gotten for me. Also when they asked me questions in class I was not able to respond to them in outsider words because I didn't know enough. Being afraid, I did not go to class again, and then they said to Roberto, "The one you have taken charge of is not coming to class."
>
> Later he said to me, "They say that you are not attending your classes."
>
> I responded, "Consider this, I really do not know the outsider words. I am afraid."
>
> Then he said, "I spoke to you the other day about the course and you said, 'I can do it.' For the sake of your people, return to your classes and learn! Then you can teach those in your village."

I said, "Okay," and I again attended my classes. But, after I had gone to my classes for about a month, I did not go anymore; when I did not learn, Roberto sent me back here. After he sent me and I had been back for a few months, he again called me and I went to Yarinacocha. He did the same thing and put me in school. However, after I had been in classes for a month or so, Roberto said to me, "Okay, at this time I shall not again live out there at the village." He stopped, and then again said, "I shall not live out there again. Another man, one who is living near my home, he will go out there. He will go out there to teach you. He will cause you to learn....Another man, with whom we will make an agreement as we go, he is coming. He is strong, a talker, and very knowledgeable. You will see. Speak in the future with those whom I will tell about you. This is what my leader told me to tell you. However, I am now leaving. Be careful. Be observant as you live with him and he teaches you in the future. All of you must treat him well in your village."

I said, "Okay," and waited for another month. After I had stayed waiting, he again sent me home.

The Cromacks left Peru in August of 1968 and we arrived sometime the next month, so we did not meet them. The Peru Branch of SIL knew in March or April of that year that we were coming and so could easily have told Robert Cromack about us and he then passed the word to Mario. All that Mario has to say about what Cromack told him was all new to me in 1994 and seems logical to me. I am not sure, however, whether his description of me as "strong, a talker, and very knowledgeable" is what he was told or is possibly something Mario introduced into the story after he had known me for twenty-five years. Thus, in 1968 we entered a very difficult situation. The original linguist was gone, the second linguist, who had gotten his Ph.D. in linguistics on the Cashinahua discourse structure, had just left, and there was a village full of unfulfilled expectations.

8

Replacements

My wife Susan and I arrived at Lima's International Airport in September 1968 just prior to a military coup that would have consequences for our entire time in Peru. When our documentation was completed, we went to the SIL center at Yarinacocha near Pucallpa for some orientation.

While there, we were told that we would be returning to Lima in a few weeks to study Spanish. We were then asked if we would consider taking over the work with the Cashinahua. I had wanted to pioneer a new group rather than build on a foundation laid by someone else. We had hoped for an assignment in the mountains, but were told that any possible allocations had been suspended because of the revolution. The political direction of the new president and his revolutionary council was unknown. So given that situation, we began to investigate how we could learn Cashinahua. We were given a few sketchy cultural studies, an approved orthography, Robert Cromack's Ph.D. dissertation on Cashinahua discourse structure, and six language lessons he had written for his wife after they married. All of Kensinger's linguistic studies were missing from the files. With these materials to study we returned to Lima for Spanish study. Unfortunately, I did not excel in Spanish, and I later learned that the Cashinahua knew very little Spanish—enough to buy and sell things. For this reason, I learned the Cashinahua language monolingually.

We were scheduled to fly out to Balta to meet the Cashinahua about the first of June 1969—"about" because the rains determine when one actually flies into the rain forest. The rains, however, did not delay us, but Susan's pregnancy did. Since she was in her first trimester, the doctor said she should not go at that time since the Purus area was malarial. She could go after that unless the malarial conditions were serious. We agreed, so I waited two or three weeks until Patrick Gray, whom we had met at jungle training camp, finished high school and could go with me. Thus, it was that Pat accompanied me on my first visit to the Cashinahua. As the wilderness training had prepared both of us for primitive living conditions, we had to deal only with the mysteries of their language and culture. At age 17, Pat had no interest in language learning. Getting by with broken Spanish, he went hunting and fishing every day, leaving me to my stumbling attempts to learn to speak the Cashinahua language.

Mario, who had been told that someone new would come, tells of our arrival as follows.

> I stayed there waiting. Then at your arrival time, which I think I was told was to be in the month of August [1968], you came. When you did not come here at that time, I stayed settled, still believing. Then when you were going to come here, I thought, "Someone says he is coming. Is it as Roberto told me?" And then I finally stood expectantly looking as the airplane was descending.
>
> Then my name, which they had told you, you were calling, "Where is Mario? Where is he? Which one is he? Where does he live?" Then I said, "As you said, I am here."
>
> Then you said, "Good. In which house will I live?"
>
> Saying, "In this house," I sent you and you lived in that house. As you lived there, I remained settled doing as I had been doing for the past several months.

I began with the language lessons that Robert Cromack had written for his wife. After I had learned the "who", "what", "when", and "where" questions, I decided I would use the Cashinahua language and elicit what I needed to say as I went along. I did not include "how" or "why" in my list of questions, because I did not know how to mark the actor of a transitive clause or even that transitivity was important. My attempts at using the "how" and "why" questions, that were in Cromack's set of lessons, drew frowns and odd or seemingly contradictory responses. These were eventually cleared up when I discovered their semantic realm for "how", and the ontological and transitive relationships signaled in the "why" questions. This study is not the place to explain these linguistic intricacies.

As Mario said, I had been given his name as the person with whom Kensinger and Cromack had worked. He was the only one who could read their language; a few, like Joaquín, could read some Spanish. At first I worked with Mario by reading aloud from whatever printed materials we had, without knowing what I was saying. He corrected my pronunciation and sometimes reread the selection so I could hear its correct rhythm and pronunciation. I also worked at learning the proper arrival and departure phrases, short often-used utterances, and the address terms I should use for each person in my growing circle of acquaintance. The people all had Hispanic names, but used these only in reference and then rarely. They regularly addressed each other by a kinship term, such as mother, father, uncle, aunt, older brother, and older sister. Beyond that, the terms are determined by ego's gender. I learned many verbs by asking, "What are you doing?" I did not know that even though the response was literally correct it also meant, "I am too busy to stop and talk with you now," as Kensinger explained in the portion of his article quoted in chapter 7.

I also spent time doing things with the men, such as group eating in the afternoon, trips by canoe, garden-plot cutting, fish drugging [poisoning], and hunting. After they got to know and trust me (after about two years), they told me to stay home while hunting because I was too big, too slow, and too clumsy. They did not get any game when I went along. I was very careful about associating with the women. I had been warned to be cautious on this issue to avoid rejection by the men. I would have liked some written guidance on this topic from the former workers because it took me some time to figure out with whom I could talk without creating problems. The key was the particular Genuine name they gave me and thus my consequent placement in their moiety-kinship system. I could be familiar with sisters and mothers but not with female cross-cousins.

Now, Pudicho's son, Grompes, comes into the story. My first clear remembrance of him is from the morning after we arrived. The airplane had just taken off and was circling over the wall of trees that shut off any view of the horizon. As I stood there gazing after my only means of departure, thinking, "What have I gotten myself into?" Grompes approached and said in Spanish, "We go to visit all the houses. You can meet all the people." And away we went.

Grompes eventually became a government-paid Health Promoter (medic), and established a clinic in his village of Balta. He later tells of his difficult road to becoming a "doctor" and how I affected his life. But first Pudicho introduces the topic of his son's becoming a "doctor".

> 66. After I came back, I have dwelt here [Balta]. I did not again go. However, later my son went also and got medicines to cure my people when they suffered pain; my son became a "doctor", a man with medicine. He is making them well. He is making my little children well. He is making the grown people well from whatever they are suffering. He is continuing to do this.

Because of the flow of topics in Pudicho's story I have only now been able to introduce Grompes' voice. His account was prompted in 1994 by my request, "Tell me about how I worked with you long ago and you became a Health Promoter." So Grompes began his narrative back when he was a young man, in order to set the scene and help me to understand that there was more to the story than just my involvement.

> By telling you about how I started to use medicine long ago, I intend to cause you to learn; listen to me.
> I was not like those who understood leaf medicines; our father [Pudicho] and our paternal grandfather's wife, these two had learned jungle plant leaves long ago. Having learned various jungle leaf medicines, they tried unsuccessfully to teach me and finally rejected me as a student. Because I had only learned a little, I tried unsuccessfully to cure those who were suffering pain, and those with a rash, and those with sores inside of the mouth, and those with swelling, and those with diarrhea.

This was at the time when he began to become enamored with the things of the outside world. The river trader, Dini Fulano, began treating Grompes as the group leader and taking him downriver to visit (Pudicho's story text block 41). Fulano is probably the outsider mentioned in the following account given by Grompes.

> Finally, an outsider also took notice of me and said, "Good. Give me some of your jungle leaf medicine also. I intend to see if it is potent." Probably he was concerned that I had not learned thoroughly, and he said, "With that being the situation, do you have lots of medicine?"
> I answered, "Not enough; my people are many. And there are lots of little children."
> Then he said, "Okay, because of that take some of ours. It was made in a factory. You can have them swallow it with water. Take only fever medicine and diarrhea medicine. You do not know enough to take others yet." That is how I started using medicines long ago. While using medicines from the outsiders, I left off using Genuine people medicines because our leaf medicines were not strong enough. I only used the medicines that various outsiders gave me. They got it from Puerto Esperanza. However, they got only aspirin and diarrhea medicine for me and I continued my normal life and work.

Then later in a different year they gave me cough medicine along with the other medicines. After I had gone and gotten these medicines, I lived in my village; causing my people to swallow medicines, I went on with my life.

I had not heard this part of his story until I taped this account. When I first knew him, he had a large family and kept a shelf full of medicines in his sleeping room. That was one reason I had the idea that he could take over the medical work that we had been doing and become an official Health Promoter. Grompes continues:

Then my friends, Ken and John, came here [Balta 1962] and I showed them the medicine. I said, "Friends, an outsider gave me medicines the other day. Take a look to see what they might be."

John said, "Where? I do not know what it is."

I said, "He said that this is diarrhea medicine."

He said, "Okay. I know that medicine. It's good," and Ken and John were watching me closely with their eyes. However, even though they were doing that, I was always causing my people to swallow medicines. When I caused them to swallow the fever medicine, I did not know anything about a [dosage] schedule for its use; with complete naiveté of thought I was causing them to swallow medicines. And I caused them to swallow diarrhea medicine and cough medicine in the same manner. Being like that I continued my normal life. I was a man without knowledge of medicines; without being concerned I made use of medicines long ago, I used medicines without instruction. At that time I mistakenly thought I knew how to use outsider medicines. As I was continuing in this manner my friend Ken finally left, going away. He had become accustomed to us; he had worked with us and then left. Then I continued my life without him.

Then my cross-cousin Mario, who had learned to read and write, said to me, "Friend, I was told that a different friend of ours shall come. I was told that he shall cause all of us to learn during the time he is with us. Roberto told me this months ago and Ken told me as he was leaving that I could do God's Word, and I could teach school and I could sell things but he prevented me from doing medicines, saying, 'Not medicines. Your cross-cousin has that.' He told me this as he was leaving the other day."

It seemed our arrival had been preceded by many expectations. And when he said, "I continued my life without him [Ken]," Grompes means providing for his own immediate and extended family—hunting, fishing, garden making, and house building and repair. Even though he had taken over from his father as the village headman, his life was much the same as that of any other good hunter, except for his coordination and arbitration functions. At first, I did not realize that he was the headman; he will emphatically point that out to me later.

His friend John is John O'Neal, the ornithologist mentioned previously. Even though there had been a denouncement against him, Kensinger was in Peru to visit his Cashinahua friends in the summer of 1968, about the time the Cromacks were leaving. Grompes relates that Mario spoke with him about our coming. Again, I do not know whether this is an accurate remembrance or possibly a story reconstructed in line with what eventually came to be. When we arrived we were not told much about Ken Kensinger. We know now that he deeply missed working with his Cashinahua friends on the Curanja River. We did not meet him until twenty-three years later. Since then he has been a great encouragement to me in my efforts to aid the Cashinahua in expressing their reactions to the outside world.

Now Grompes does exactly what I requested when I spoke to him about recording his story. I told him to be perfectly candid about what he thought of me back then, and he is.

> I thought about Mario's words while continuing to live here. Even though another friend was coming, I was causing those who suffered pain to swallow medicine as I lived here. Then at a different time, a different year also, my new friend came. When my friend came, I thought, "What type of person is he who came today? What is he like?" I looked, "True, he is a man." After he and the tall teenager [Pat Gray] who came with him to us, had arrived, I spoke with them. He did not yet know what I was like, and I also did not know what he was like either. Then the next day, when I assumed he would be coming regularly by airplane, I thought, "I will cause him to meet my people so that he would become accustomed to all of them." Then I took him all around the village, starting to cause him to meet my people. As I was taking him to where each of our people lived, I was saying, "This one is a father. This one is an uncle. This one is an aunt." I did this going all around the village; I did this in outsider words because he did not yet know Genuine peoples' words.

During that first month in Balta I found Grompes helpful and friendly, but observed no obvious indications to me that he was the village headman. As Mario said, I had been told that Kensinger and Cromack had worked with him, so I found it natural to work with Mario. Even after Grompes and I scouted the area at the downriver end of the 300-meter airstrip with the idea of lengthening it, I did not realize he held any special position. We discovered that we could easily add fifty meters to its length. The pilot, Ted Long, had told me that the strip was a bit short, even for the Helicourier STOL (short take-off and landing) airplane. He said that once, during a take off, he had flown right through the banana plants just across the little stream at the upriver end of the airstrip.

Thus, when I asked the Cashinahua men to cut, clear, and level this additional fifty meters, I worked through Mario. I learned that there were moieties, and that all the men were either Children of Radiance or Children of Jaguar (the word means "carnivore" but "Jaguar" is the head of that category). So I asked the men who wanted to work to form two work teams based on moiety, with Mario leading the Children of Radiance and Grompes leading the Children of Jaguar. This enabled them to work alternating days on the airstrip, while continuing their hunting and garden preparations. This system, which was very rational from my point of view, worked well. I remember saying to Mario, "It is like you are the leader of the Children of Radiance and Grompes is the leader of the Children of Jaguar." He gave me an odd look, but did not correct me. Those early days of language learning were like running through a forest in a fog. All the trees are blurred, and some trees become clear as one approaches, but then blur again as one passes on. I remember understanding situations in which I was directly involved, but having no ability to understand what was going on around me or what was not spoken directly to me.

Grompes now tells of his reaction to my presumptions and misunderstanding.

> After living with us for several months, he finally called his wife. She came by airplane and descended onto our airstrip. After she came she lived with him. I myself did not know much about them; I was not yet reciprocally friends with them. And I thought, "They are befriending my cousin Mario only. Maybe it is because he is the school doer; maybe it is because he knows how to read; maybe it is because he knows how to write, that they think he is the leader of this village. They think Mario is the parent of this place. Okay, they are looking around and do not know who I am yet."

Even though that was the situation, I was the second person that they took to Yarinacocha so I could get the medical knowledge that I continually use now [1994]. It was there by talking with him that I befriended him.

However, when he had just come, he said to me, "Okay, have Mario do this limited amount of medical work."

Then later Mario said to him, "I listened to you the other day and have done the medical work. However, by myself I cannot do it." Mario then came to me and said, "I spoke to him about you yesterday. Maybe you are able to handle the medicines he brings. Let's see how things go for the time being."

Thinking of what he said, I stayed here and continued my normal way of life. Then a letter came for my cousin Mario and Ricardo that said, "Good. Mario, they are calling you from Esperanza. Go and come back. Go and talk with them for a short time and then come back quickly."

However, Mario responded, "I don't know. Maybe I am afraid of the outsiders. No, it is not that. Friend, I am not the real leader of this village."

Ricardo asked, "Who is the village leader?"

Mario answered, "Grompes is the village leader."

Then Ricardo said, "Good. Tell him that he should go."

Mario went and told me what was said and added, "Listen to him for the time being."

Then I went to where my friend Ricardo was and said, "How is it with the outsiders?"

He said to me, "Okay, are you the village leader?"

I answered, "Yes, I am the parent of this place."

He took my hand in his and shook it saying, "Good. An outsider is calling you." And I went.

After the same one had spoken with only me, I went. I had traveled for several days, continually hearing outsider words and upon arriving at far away Puerto Esperanza, they made me stay, asking, "What are your friends, who keep coming and going, teaching you all?"

I said, "They are teaching us about schools. They are teaching us how we should live. And they are learning our words."

Then they [sic] said, "Good. I shall go see for myself. Go home now. I shall go and visit you later." I slept three nights while coming before I entered my village and met Ricardo.

He asked, "How was your trip?"

I answered, "They talked to me the other day. The outsiders spoke about you and I calmed them down by telling them about what you are doing." Then I continued on a different topic, saying, "Okay Ricardo, even though our people treated you and also Mario as village leaders, you made a mistake the other day. I have been the village leader here for a long time; you also, when you tried to act as leader, you made a mistake the other day. Okay, things should continue as they were before you came, with me as leader."

I remember this incident much the way Grompes does; he had to tell me point blank that he was the leader. I had made the mistake of many investigators. I had come with an idea of what governance was, which then blinded me to the reality among the Cashinahua. I had drawn conclusions based on what I saw, apart from considering the abstract aspects of culture, which can be learned mostly through language. This was not my last mistake based on my own preconceived ideas, even though I had theoretically been instructed to look for concepts radically different from our own. To say the least, from then on I discussed all my ideas with Grompes first, even keeping him informed concerning the later developments in the schools.

Susan came to Balta after we determined that there was no longer malaria in the area. I learned later that a year or so before, a UNESCO malaria control team from Brazil had come up the Purús River and was fortunate enough to contact nearly 100 percent of the inhabitants of the headwater's basin. The Cashinahua told me that the team treated everyone with bitter medicine, and sprayed all the houses. The treatment must have been thorough and effective. I have not heard of a single case of malaria in the entire region in the past thirty years.

The conversations Grompes reports about speaking with the officials in Puerto Esperanza concerning us and about Mario doing medical work probably took place during our second or third year. We did not have the beginnings of a school until 1970 and I did not leave any medicines, aspirin, or antidiarrhea medicine with Mario until toward the end of 1970 when I returned to Yarinacocha. This does not mean Grompes is mistaken. He just compressed the past into time blocks in accordance with the past time categories of his language.[10]

---

[10]There are six categories of past tense, with six different suffixes, ranging from a long time ago, one year back, a month ago, yesterday, sometime today, and a little while ago. These are not used in a strict manner but depend, for example, on how fresh they want to convey a memory is to them, or to indicate a relative time within the time frame an action took place in reference to the time of speaking.

The Cashinahua past time categories also affect the memory of events; the category "long ago" (5 or more years) is often compressed, like the American term "once upon a time". Grompes has combined conversations and concepts from our first two or so years, 1969–1971, to express his remembrances of the three-way relationship between himself, Mario, and me. This was the period of time before Grompes started going to Yarinacocha to study, and I entered into the life of a place where he was "Place Parent", their word for headman. The people in Cashinahua villages appear to be doing as they please in fulfilling their roles. However, the men keep the *Xanen ibu* 'Place Parent' informed of what they are doing or where they are going. Also, the *Xanen ibu*'s wives keep their eyes and ears open so they can keep him informed of what is going on in the female realm. This is part of his subtle function as arbitrator and coordinator; as Place Parent he feels responsible for all who live there.

It was during that first year that Grompes changed my Genuine name. When I first arrived I had been given the name *Yawa Bichi* 'Peccary Skin'. This made me 'Child of Jaguar' so people could relate to me with kinship terms. Later when my wife had arrived someone named her *Badi Butuani* 'Sun Descended Long Ago', which made her 'Child of Radiance'. As far as we understood, our marriage was proper in their cultural context because we were of different moieties. Then Grompes told us that our marriage was a bit wrong, so that he had to change my name to make our relationship correct. Even though we were of different moieties which is correct, we were at different generational levels, which is a bit wrong. He then made me a namesake of his by changing my name to *Punu Bena* 'New Muscle', thus placing me in the same alternating generational level as Susan.[11]

Within a month Susan had caught up to me in language learning; they were able to play a joke on us because of my name. We had learned that the word *ain* meant 'wife'. One day one of the men began to point at different women in the village, saying to the two of us concerning me, "That's his *ain*. That's his *ain*. That's his *ain*. And that's his *ain*." As he chuckled, Susan said to me in English, "What have you been doing out here while I was at Yarina?" Of course, I had no answer. As it turned out, the root meaning of the word *ain* is male ego's female first cross-cousin, someone in the correct generational level marriage section of the other moiety. It is also used, however, to mean 'wife' because that is the group from which wives ideally come. Susan was in that group with all those he had pointed out. The same relationship holds for the word *bene* which means female ego's male first cross-cousin, but is also used to indicate 'husband'. By

---

[11] For further discussion and explanation of Cashinahua moieties A and B and alternating generational namesake groups which also function as ideal marriage sections, see Kensinger 1995:101–130.

adjusting my name to 'New Muscle' and making me one of his namesakes, Grompes was also indicating that he wanted an equal relationship with me. This also gave him the opportunity to have more influence on me.

Many relationships were initiated during that first stay in the village of Balta, and they either matured into closer friendships or dissolved as the people realized that we could not meet all their needs and expectations. By necessity we were going to be doing linguistic investigation and aiding in the setting up of bilingual schools. These were the jobs specified in our contract with the Ministry of Education. However, we were also drawn into many activities as advocates for the Cashinahua people as they sought to deal with Peruvian outsiders on a more equal footing. The additional areas in which we involved ourselves were: adult education, health care, mercantile relationships, community development projects, and official documentation, both community and personal. All of these have had an effect on their culture. As I look back, I see that these activities were necessary to support our personal goal of translating portions of the Bible into their language. Following are some long accounts by Mario and Grompes, which relate how the people were affected by these activities and the changes that took place during the 1970s and 80s.

Ordinarily, SIL linguists in Peru do not get involved with teachers and school books until they have learned to speak and understand their language and demonstrate that they can handle the basic grammar. However, we had stepped into an existing situation where Mario and the community already had high expectations of having a school. Mario continues by relating a conversation he says we had the first year, with me speaking first.

> Later you asked me, "Okay, do you always teach?"
> And I said, "Yes, I always teach. However, you can teach me, just as they told me you would months ago."
> Then you said, "Good. In that case, I will think about you becoming a teacher for the time being."
> And while you were thinking about me, I was also thinking about you, "I wonder how he is going to teach."

As with almost all remembered conversations, this is a condensed version of several conversations that took place over many days. After I had been studying the language with Mario for about two months, Mario mentioned that he had studied at Yarinacocha, and that Roberto (Cromack) had promised that he could be a schoolteacher. I did not know how long ago he had studied, but he read and wrote well in his own language and conversed with the various river traders with apparent ease. At first, I told him we could not set up a school because we had neither primers nor permission. The next time he brought up the subject he told me that Professor Tapia, the head of the bilingual school course, was his friend and that he would give his permission. We also knew that there were two or three drafted primers in the files that had been started by Gail Cromack. I then found out by radio that there was a preliminary preparation class going on that Mario could enter if he went to Yarinacocha with us in September. Things were rushing at us too quickly, but Susan and I talked it over and decided we would give it a try. We did not know how difficult it would be.

Mario continues:

> Thinking about me, you started teaching me long ago. Later, two months maybe, while you were learning our words, you said to me, "Okay, it is good. When I go, I will take you. Go with me in the future. I will put you in school and then start working with you in January."
>
> Then I thought, "Good. This one is my very good friend. He is strong-willed. He has the outsiders' words. He can help me with reading and writing." Thinking this, I was happy as I stayed here. Later during September my friend, and his wife, and my paternal nephew Herman and I, we went to Yarinacocha by airplane. I was happy there, thinking, "It is good that you put me into class, doing as Roberto had done for me months and months ago." However, because I mistakenly thought that you could order me to leave whenever you wanted to and because I was afraid of them at school, I said to you, "I cannot do it."
>
> But you said, "Do it. Learn it. You can teach in your village. You are able to help them to learn." Because you said that, you made me learn. I did not learn only at school. By repeatedly taking me to where our fellow believers were meeting, where our friends gathered in Puerto Callao, you also caused me to learn; you did it for months. There also I did not know anything, just as when Belisario first tried to teach us about God. Thinking of that while I was at the meetings, I started to learn the good news about Christ Jesus.
>
> While I was living in that manner, various ones at school said to me, "We assume that you are not able to learn."
>
> I thought, "I am not as they say," and you kept saying to me, "Learn." You did not do it slowly; doing it like you were teaching your own real child, you taught me thoroughly.

> While demonstrating and saying, "Like this, one is able to do it," you pushed me along in school long ago.

As Mario said, I am strong-willed, and when Mario tried to back out as he had done with Robert Cromack, I did not let him get away with it. Besides, I had committed myself prematurely to preparing for a school and was too stubborn to back out. As Mario had said, Professor Tapia knew him and greeted him by name, putting him in the preparatory class the next day. I did not work directly with Mario very much until January, because Susan and I were in a language learning workshop with Mario's cousin Herman as our assistant. One thing that helped us greatly with our continued language learning was to have both Mario and Herman sleeping upstairs in our house and eating with us. Treating them as family, which is how they expect to be treated when they visit relatives in other villages, enabled us to use their language continually. (Herman is one of the few who to this day will correct me when he feels I have said something incorrectly.)

I do not remember Mario's telling me about anyone's comments denigrating his learning ability, but I do not doubt it, and I did strongly encourage him. I told him that if he did his mathematics well and pronounced Spanish words well, the professors would think he was intelligent and that he could learn the meanings of the words as he went along. Then because he knew him, Professor Tapia put Mario in the regular course in January, even though he lacked a birth certificate and a second grade certificate.

At this same time Susan found the two or three draft primers in the files and began consulting with those linguists who spoke cognate Panoan languages. She was able to produce starting primers, even though we did not speak the language very well. I continued to study with Herman and helped Mario with his lessons in the evenings. Mario continues:

> And then because I pulled good grades the first year [1970], I started teaching after I returned to Balta. When the government was not paying me yet, you gave me a little bit of money irregularly as time passed. And when I went to study the second year, 1971, I did not have personal documents nor an appointment to have an official school and I was preoccupied with my sad situation.
>
> Even though it was that way, even though you, by force of will, were not able to make the outsiders do it, our friend, the good man Professor Tapia, the Coordinator of Bilingual Schools who lived there, helped me with my personal documents. He always helped each of the native villages to have a teacher.

I wish it had been as easy as Mario said. In Peru an individual is not a legal citizen until he/she has personal documents. Just as we had Ministry of Education I.D. cards, everyone must carry documents, presenting them when requested. For Peru, the fundamental document is a birth certificate. However, in the Cashinahua way of thinking, a Cashinahua has identity if he/she has a Genuine name and relatives to vouch for that name. If a baby is unnamed it is not a person, thus is subject to infanticide, as was illustrated in Nacimiento's account in chapter 2. Mario was now interacting with another culture in which he could not simply claim his Hispanic name and have it vouched for. He needed a document—a piece of paper—a conceptual change that would eventually affect every Cashinahua in Peru.

Professor Tapia advised me to seek out a "friend" who had connections in whatever ministry I wanted to deal with. He then introduced me to a person who could help obtain a Supplemental Birth Certificate for Mario. This process involves having someone with a full set of documents certify that the person without a Birth Certificate is a resident of Peru and is who he/she says he/she is. Fortunately, one of the river traders from the Purús region was in Pucallpa and signed for Mario. Later, when Mario had his documents he could sign for the other Cashinahua. But it was a long process.

At about this time, during our second extended stay in Balta, I came to the realization that the medical work we were doing was a wonderful aid to language learning. If we did not detach ourselves from it, however, we would not have time for anything else. In addition, when we left Balta, I left only a few medicines with Mario, who could read directions but did not have proper training. Furthermore, he had to be away to continue his studies for the first three months of each year. It was then that I had the idea that Grompes might be able to learn enough Spanish to enter a low-level medical training course even though he was in his mid-30s, and already a grandfather.

This is how Grompes tells what happened (he had just told me that he was the headman and that I should keep it in mind).

> After I had spoken to him that way, I stayed settled in my village for several months. Then my friend finally asked me, "Do you always handle medicines?"
>
> I answered, "Yes, I always handle my leaf medicines."
>
> He continued, "Not that. Do you always handle outsider medicines?"
>
> I answered, "I always handle them."

Then he said, "Good. May I cause you to learn about outsider medicines sometime in the future?"

I said, "I can do it."

He said, "Good. Do you write?"

I said, "No, I never learned to write."

Then he said, "How can that be? You are a village leader. Those who are leaders can write. You must learn to write. Didn't Mario ever teach you to write?"

I answered, "Even though he taught me, I never learned."

He thought and said, "Okay, may I teach you?"

I said, "Yes, teach me."

He said, "Good. Come back when the sun is setting."

I said, "Good," and left.

Later when the sun was setting, I again came to his house, and he said, "How goes it? Write something for me now."

My friend, the man, did not do it. The wife gave me the word syllables to write. She said, "May I show you how to write?" and wrote each syllable for me. However, I was afraid because I was very slow. I was not able to do it in front of her; I wanted to do it where she couldn't see me. But she said, "Don't do that. Do it this way. Write it."

I thought, "Okay, how may I do it?" And even though I was afraid, my heart said, "It's all right." I myself was afraid and thought in my heart, "It's all right." Because of that I said, "I will do it. Write it for me." I tried to copy what she wrote for me; I worked at it very, very slowly, thinking, "I myself, I am now grown up. I am now a grown man. I have lots of children. Even though I am not able to learn, even though I am that way, my thinking is good," then I followed what she drew for me; at my house I continued to follow her examples. But the result was, I was doing it badly.

Then after three sleeps, she called me and I went to her house. She said, "Now that you have stored in your head what I wrote for you the other day, by means of your thinking, you yourself write it, remembering with your head."

I tried to do it but I did not remember, so I tried to sneak a look at my notebook. But Ricardo said, "Don't touch it! Store it in your head and then do it yourself." So I wrote it, only not correctly. Then he said, "You're a grown man. You must learn. You're the village leader; learn to read and write."

I thought, "Okay, I tried to learn and I am not learning. I am suffering a lot of anguish. While suffering a lot, how may

I act?" I figuratively threw them away and left for my house. There I fell asleep and upon awakening in the morning, I thought, "Truly, I am good. I can learn. Will I live poorly without learning the writing? Can I live well with writing?" Then I said to my wife, "It is good. I am going to learn writing," and again went to their house.

Then he said, "How is it with you? First, read these." Doing it, I was doing it hesitantly, when he said, "Don't do it that way."

I thought, "That's okay." and by means of my memory I read his letters out loud, "B? A? C? D?" doing it in a questioning manner.

He said, "Don't do it that way! This one word only, quickly tell it out loud."

I thought, "I do not fear him. What may I do?"

Then with strong words he said, "Do it! You are a man. Learn it now!"

I was very fearful. At that time, one time only, I was afraid. I was thinking, "Now I am afraid. Sigh, how should I act?"

Then my paternal-cousin, Kunin Chapu [Joaquín], who had gone downriver to be among the outsiders two or three years before and whose brother had told him to come home, he helped me learn, saying, "Older Brother, may I tell you the letter?"

I said, "Tell me."

Demonstrating, he said, "This letter, do it this way. Like this doing, write it here."

The wife caught sight of what he was doing and said to my cousin, "Don't touch his writing. You do not teach. Don't touch his. Do only yours, that which I assigned you."

He did not tell me the letters again, and even though I had read the letters hesitantly days before, I stayed in my house for five days studying the letters. I did not come here to your house for five days. Then I started to learn the letters. I was thinking, "I assumed I was able to say 'A' thusly. 'A' and 'B' and 'D', I was doing when he stopped me. Thus I assumed that I need to say complete words out loud." Saying, "This word, is it 'fish'?" I started long ago. By means of the word 'fish' I got it; I caught onto saying whole written words. "Is it 'fish'?" was all I got. Again I slept and on the sixth day I thought, "Now I have completely got it."

After I had completely got it, I went to their house. Again my friend, the woman, asked me, "Do it. Read it right along." I read it right along completely. Then she said, "Wow, good. Who told you? Ricardo maybe? What, ha ha?"

But I said, "It was not that way. It was you. You caused me to learn." Then everything was very good between the two of us, and I was happy.

Then she said, "Do what you have now learned. You, yourself, write what you have learned."

I slowly did it. As I was slowly writing, they did not talk to me. Thinking, "Ah, good," they watched me in silence.

And I was thinking, "Finally I have learned. I have now learned an entire word." I had learned an entire word. I was not afraid of him any more. I continued to think, "I can do it. I myself, I can do it. Even though I am doing it, I am doing it almost correctly, only lacking a little." I did not learn completely each of the corrections that they made. Doing well and learning, I lived my normal life.

As I remember those difficult times, Grompes was always the self-assured leader, the man who had politely but firmly corrected me the year before. Whenever I have worked with him I have always gotten the distinct impression that I was working with someone more intelligent than I. That was one reason I wanted him to be the Health Promoter. Furthermore, he was the only one with the authority to later tell them which medicines were needed for which conditions. (The lack of maturity and authority makes it difficult for a young person to be either a health promoter or teacher among the indigenous groups of Amazonia.) I never knew until 1994 the difficulties he had had. All I remember was his hard work as he struggled with the concept of written words and groups of words. This was a large cultural shift for him, a man about thirty-four years old, a village headman, the husband of three wives, and the father of thirteen children. It was not easy for him to be a student. But when he learned to read and write, he set a standard for the other men which paid dividends later on.

9
Accelerated Change

At about that time, since Mario was busy teaching, I needed someone else to study with. I had not been able to settle on any one, and my relationship with Herman had disintegrated. I had persisted in using a systematic, step-by-step set of procedures to discover linguistic categories by setting up replacement frames. This turned out to be a disaster for both of us. And whenever I asked various people how my language learning was coming along, they always answered, "Good. You are speaking well."

Then Susan suggested I ask Marcelino, Pudicho's son-in-law. So I found Marcelino and asked him how he thought my language learning was coming along. He said, "Terrible. But I can help you." He turned out to be a tremendous help to us. He had worked for years in Brazil tapping rubber and was not impressed nor awed by outsiders. He never let me slip by with a mistake, and when he realized that there was money to be made, he learned to read and write his own language in one month. He was not afraid of the concept, he was not a child. There are only eighteen letters that are basically always pronounced the same way. He sat down, memorized them, and copied them into notebooks by syllable types. The only problem we had at first was that because he was a very good hunter, he did not have the time I needed. He and his brothers were working together to buy a motor; they were tired of poling their canoes, especially upstream. At that time, in the early 1970s, Señor Gamboa was paying top prices for jaguar, ocelot, nutria, and peccary skins and was liberal with the Cashinahua because they paid their debts. Belisario expresses their attitude concerning the need for outside things when he continues the story of his life after he moved to Balta.

Later I was thinking about outsider things and feeling deprived while poling my canoe downriver during the flood season. I had to alternately pole and paddle where it was deep, which made it difficult traveling. I was suffering like an animal when I met an outsider traveling easily upriver using a motor. I said to myself, "I intend to get a motor." Then I went to make an agreement pact with an outsider and said to him, "I want to get a motor."

He said, "Okay, but a big motor is very expensive. I can't give you what you want. But you can get a smaller six horse-power motor; that I can give you." That which I had spoken about and asked for, he wrote in his ledger and several months later he brought a motor to me. Along with the men in my household I got it and paid for it over the next several months. Now by means of it I travel on the river, no poling. I no longer pole to go someplace; going downriver and going upriver I always travel by means of my motor.

Then following that, the next year we did not collect rubber again; we started hunting for skins as our work to get things. A year later after they had changed to taking skins, I got a sewing machine for my wives. When I got a sewing machine, it wasn't just me. We all got motors, sewing machines, and a variety of other expensive outsider things.

After we got things we were no longer suffering like animals without things as we used to. When we came downriver the outsiders cheated us because we did not know anything; in vain we collected rubber, losing our labor. Then later other different outsiders came and are now teaching us everything. We are no longer ignorant, we are learning and living well.

We were those different outsiders. Belisario was speaking of the good times in the early 1970s when they were getting the things they wanted. This was the recurring theme since the opening section of Pudicho's narrative. The Cashinahua wanted an outsider trader who would treat them on an equal basis, something like the reciprocal concept their ancestors had functioned with. Within their group, one person would give something of value and the other person would reciprocate later. There was no need to keep a strict account because it was all among relatives or classificatory relatives. This was how they first interacted with the traders. They gave rubber and then later the trader brought them things. But the reciprocation was not equal. All of the river traders wanted to make money and

Accelerated Change 119

Señor Ladislao Gamboa, mentioned by Pudicho's brother Idiodoro, was no exception. He became the dominant trader of the group working on the Purús River in Peru during the 1960s and 70s. However, even though he charged the same high prices as the other traders for the things brought in from the outside, he came to trust the Cashinahua. And he advanced them more credit than he did the other indigenous groups, did not bring alcohol, and would invite them to eat at his table when they were in Puerto Esperanza. Thus, they liked him because they were getting things and he treated them fairly. Later on, when the prices for skins began to fall in the mid-1970s, Gamboa took his earnings and opened an import-export business in Pucallpa.

Because he and his brothers had paid for their motor, Marcelino had more time to help me. But as I worked with him my priority was still to continue to push Grompes along toward taking over the medical work. He relates it as follows.

> Then at the time Ricardo was again going to go to Yarinacocha, he obligated me saying, "Friend, do you always handle medicine?"
> I answered, "I always handle it."
> He said, "Good. Have you now learned?"
> I responded, "I am always learning. I always cause them to swallow medicine."
> Then he said, "Okay, would you like to go to our house over in the direction of the Ucayali?"
> I said, "I can go. I went with Ken long ago and was happy. I can go."
> And he said, "Good. I can take you."
> My thinking was raised up in joy and I thought, "Good. He said I shall go." Then I said, "Friend, you have said that I can go."
> And he said, "Good. Go in the future and return."
> I said, "Good." Later I again went to their house and filled a notebook with another lesson which they had written out for me the day before. In front of him I quickly filled the notebook. In front of his eyes I filled it.
> Then he said, "Read it completely out loud." So I read it completely out loud for them.
> He said, "Good. Now read these that I am mixing for you," and he wrote, *BAN, BIN,* and *BEN.* I learned to read them completely. After I had learned those completely, I did not have to do those again. Next he wrote, *CHE, CHI,* and various

other ones like these for me and I learned to read them out loud.

Then I thought, "Okay, I have not learned the outsiders' words. I am only learning ours at this time." Then I asked him about it, saying, "Do outsider words for me also."

He responded, "No, not now. First learn to read and write your words completely. Then in the same way when you study the outsider words, the letters shall come out the same way as they do now."

So I said, "Okay," and stayed settled for about a month. I was not afraid to go because I had the impression of writing in my head.

When he was going, he promised me, saying, "Go to Yarinacocha as I promised you months ago."

I said, "Good," and went with my wife by means of an airplane. But before I went I asked him, "For how long am I going this time, I mean in reference to what you said the other day?"

He answered, "Go for nine months. Your maternal nephew Herman has gone ahead of you. Go and work with him."

I said, "Okay," and went. However, my reading and writing were very weak, and even though I was very slow, by repeatedly going to Spanish classes, I was slowly learning the outsiders' words. After I had spent nine months and was ready to come home, he sent me back to Balta.

I cannot remember all the comings and goings by airplane at that time, but I was satisfied that Grompes was reading and writing his own language well. He later was a wonderful role model for all the children who stayed in school and struggled with what was for them an alien practice of drawing words on paper. When they saw their village leader and many young men reading and writing their own language, the children continued their studies because it had become an adult thing to do. I never actually taught an adult literacy class, except with Grompes, but before many primers were available, I made flash cards with each possible syllable type. Then with Mario's and Joaquín's help, we weeded out the ones they thought were not used in their language. These cards also had sample words on the reverse side. They were then used informally during the first two years by some of the 20- to 30-year-old men to learn to read and write (Mario says there were also some young women). I was then able to use the following strategy to encourage reading and writing among the adult men. Up until then I had made a list of things they wanted me to buy for them in Pucallpa, where prices were about one-third the river trader prices. I told them that I would not take their requests for things to buy unless they could write it on a piece of paper. Suddenly, there was a lot of teaching and learning going on and the notes poured in. In this way, I was able to establish a need in their minds for reading and writing.

I did not have the time nor the ability to teach Grompes to improve his Spanish, so I sent him to study Spanish in a course at the bilingual school facility. This school was normally used to help prepare candidates to study to be teachers, but Professor Tapia was again kind and placed Grompes in the class to prepare him for the medical course. He began in April 1971, and during the course's nine months I was either in Balta or in a linguistic workshop, so did not check on him very closely. Then because he was chosen to go to Lima for the twenty-fifth anniversary celebration of the Summer Institute of Linguistics' work in Peru, I assumed he was doing well in Spanish. My hope at that time was to convince the three nurses who ran the Health Promoter course for the regional hospital that someone much older than most of the students, and without any formal schooling could do the work. They were skeptical of me and doubtful about Grompes. In order to get their approval, I had to promise to attend classes with him so I could help him study in the evenings. He was set to start the Health Promoter course in April 1972. So in January, I sent Grompes and his wife to Balta on the airplane that came to take Mario out to Pucallpa for his continuing education. I told them to wait in Balta for the airplane that would take Mario back there at the end of March or early April.

Grompes now tells of one of the most difficult times in our relationship. Grompes and his wife Natalia were staying at our house during the course, and during his first week of study, I was heavily involved in the final week of a Panoan linguistic workshop.

> After I had come back by airplane, my people were asking me, "How well have you learned?"
>
> I told them, "I am returning from learning outsiders' words. I shall go again and get medicines for you."
>
> Mistakenly thinking that everything was well and that it would be easy to study the medicines, I again went to Yarinacocha. After I had again gone, Ricardo put me into the medical course. When he enrolled me, I entered thinking incorrectly that all was well. However, when they wrote there on the blackboard, I tried to learn but I went soft. I myself, I was not soft. I was strong. My thinking went soft. I was writing it very slowly in my notebook. I was very slow when the teacher asked who had finished. Those who had entered the

course with me raised their hands; however, I did not want to raise my hand.

The nurses said to me, "How goes it? Okay, you are not a turtle. You must learn faster. A turtle is slow, but a person can learn quickly. We assume that you do not write very often."

I answered, "Even though I can write, I am not able to do the lesson."

One of them said, "Even though it is that way, do it." Three very beautiful women taught me long ago. Their names were Joy, and Juana, and Wilma; they taught me. One of them taught and another wrote on the blackboard, saying, "Do like this." The symptoms that someone had and what to do for them, I did not write and learn. Again one of them said to me, "Okay, at your house ask your friend. Your friend can tell you by means of your words."

That was good. I was happy. But when I came and entered his house and said, "Friend, this is what they told me today."

He said, "Good. What?"

I asked, "What is this?" I, the very same one, asked about it.

He said, "I can't do it. It's yours. You learn it."

Again not being able to do that, I was suffering. Finally, a very little bit crossed over to me. When that happened, I thought, "It's good."

Then the next day they gave me an exam on that which they had written out, saying, "Write what you learned yesterday, the illness you learned about yesterday—what you learned about diarrhea and why someone hurts that way."

On the way to the house I was thinking, "Okay. I have tried to learn and it has not entered my head."

Then Ricardo said, "Friend, how goes it in class?"

I said, "How am I able to do it? This outsider told me to write out answers to this exam. Do it for me. I will copy it later."

But he said, "Don't do it that way. I will not do it for you. Learn it yourself."

I thought, "Oh my, what should I do now?" and I did not sleep that night.

After not sleeping, I went to class in that condition, and the nurse said, "Give us the take-home exams now." The knowledgeable ones gave them their papers all around the room;

> however, I had not written on the paper they had given me. Then one of the nurses said, "This is bad. I have not taught you anything. Your friends are knowledgeable. They are the ones who must cause you to learn."
> I again came to their house and asked about the exam. My friend, the woman, said, "You are not a bad student. To do it well, do not write long answers. Write each of these points. Write two words, that's all, and learn them at this time. When you have learned these completely, then you will be able to understand all of it."
> Studying only that, looking at only those points, I did not sleep; with only my eyes I stayed awake all night.
> The next morning, my friend, the woman, asked, "Did you sleep well last night?"
> I lied, saying, "Yes, I fell asleep last night." Even though I did not sleep, I went to class and did the exam. And finally I pulled out a good mark.
> One of the nurses said, "Wow, now you have done it. Good." Then she told my friends by telephone, "Your friend Grompes is now learning," and they sent me to my friends' house.
> When I had entered, they asked, "Have you now learned?"
> I responded, "I have now learned something."
> They each said, "Good. I am happy for you."

This all took place during the first week, and I had no idea of his distress. I had asked Susan to help him while I worked day and night with Marcelino to finish a linguistics paper. Then when I started going to class with him I discovered the challenge before us. Grompes continues:

> So with much suffering, I had finally gotten a little bit of their teaching. At first only my friend, the woman, helped me by going to various classes with me. Later, my friend Ricardo helped me after he had finished his other work; he went with me repeatedly each day to where they were teaching me. He sat with me and when I did not understand what the women were teaching and writing on the blackboard, my friend would whisper, "It is their word for *chixua* (diarrhea). Write it." By means of our words he repeatedly told me whatever I did not understand; not only that, when I did not understand the various illnesses they were writing on the blackboard for me, he told me by means of our words and I wrote them in my notebook repeatedly long ago. Also at his house in the

evenings, we talked about whatever they taught us that day; we were learning by asking each other as we spoke long ago.

At first, he was teaching only me, and then a week or so later, I told my friend Ricardo about my friend Lucho, of the Machiguenga tribe, who was suffering because there was not anyone to help him. He said, "Good. In order for me to teach him along with you, bring him tomorrow." And I brought him the next evening and I studied with Lucho. Whenever we made a mistake, my friend corrected us, teaching by means of strong words; with much difficulty we learned the names of many various outsider medicines. I was studying so hard that my body became like it was feverish, my skin became hot and I thought, "I am not able to go in any direction. I am frustrated in escaping to anywhere, there is no trail. I am frustrated in going upriver; I am frustrated in going upriver on the Ucayali." I was frustrated in telling my friend how I felt. I could not tell him; I thought that he would hit me. I did not tell him. I really did not tell him. Being afraid of him, suffering a lot, I again pulled good marks; again I did not make mistakes on exams.

My friend, the woman, said to me, "Good. Now it is good. Friend, did you pull a perfect 20 today?"

I answered, "Yes, they gave me a perfect mark of 20 today." She was very satisfied.

After they finished teaching us at Yarinacocha, they took Lucho and me along with the knowledgeable ones to the government hospital in Pucallpa because we had pulled good marks. There they only asked us a little bit about patient medical forms and medicine inventory forms. Those who were there at the hospital gave me a small amount of money; it was 18,000 soles that they gave me.

His recollections are good. Both Grompes and Lucho were poorly prepared academically for the course, so I attended all their classes after the first week and studied with them in the evenings. I found I had to drill them and have them learn by rote the symptoms and treatments for each condition. They did not need the full training of a medical doctor, but they did learn the relationship between certain medical conditions and the regimens of medicine listed in their manuals. They used their manuals much like a cookbook. The course taught them to treat people's illnesses, but as Grompes indicated, it did not put much emphasis on the paperwork and reporting processes. Indigenous people, like Grompes, from cultures

Accelerated Change 125

without a literate tradition do not understand the need for records on paper. Grompes continues, as he tells of setting up his clinic.

> After I got the money, I came home from there and did not go again; I finally had medicine at my house. I myself had caused myself to suffer difficulty. They did not suffer difficulty; I myself was preoccupied, suffering difficulty. Being very preoccupied, I came and descended to the village by airplane. I brought the medicine that they gave me at the hospital; arriving at my village I was happy. I was not happy at the course; I had worked with fear. However, when I had come home I was not afraid anymore. I told my people, "Good. What I heard in the past days, I now know." My people were happy with me. So that they would continue to be happy and think, "Good. Now he is a man with medical knowledge," I caused them to swallow medicine, and I gave them injections as they had taught me. I was doing patient examinations as they had taught me, asking them, "What hurts? How did you start to hurt the other day?" Doing this to them, I did continually what I had finally learned months before. I lived in my village doing what I had learned months before. However, I had learned only a very little bit about the medical report documents. I had learned only a little and when my reports went repeatedly to the hospital, some were bad, on some I made mistakes, and some were good. Because of that, the ones who gave me money had only contracted me, and the director of the Pucallpa hospital was saying, "Okay, because he is only on a contracted basis, he should be terminated." But my friend was thinking of me and said to the hospital director, "It cannot be that way. He is a Genuine man, the leader of his village. His thinking is good, and when he does his report forms, he is doing them better. Don't give up on him. Don't throw him out of the program. He is always working in his village. Please continue to help him in his village." By doing this, the outsider listened to him and did not terminate me, saying, "Okay," to Ricardo. Then my friend left me, going away.

At the medical course Grompes displayed an air of self control and confidence which was part of being a headman, but, as he reveals, he was out of his element. When he returned to his village, his ability with medicines enhanced his position in the village. However, while Grompes was gone for Spanish study and the medical training, his other father, Pudicho's brother Belisario, assumed the functions of headman and felt he should continue after Grompes came back. At the time I saw no discord between them, but years later Grompes told me that he did not challenge his uncle but waited, and slowly the people began to consult him again as the *Xanen ibu* 'Place Parent'. Thus, by consensus he returned to his previous functions.

Grompes has more to say about my relationship to him and the clinic.

> When he had not left yet, I was concerned about the small amount of money they were giving me; I was continually receiving it without understanding the system. At first I did not know how to count money. Getting the money for me, my friend got me a motor to propel a canoe. After he got the motor, he said to me, "This is it, friend. You can try it out. Now that you have started to work, and because I have confidence that you will continue to work and they will pay you, I used my own money to get this motor for you the other day."
>
> Then I said, "That seems good to me. I do not understand motors yet; it is good." I got it long ago. After I got it, I incorporated it into my life and I was handling medicines to make my people well. When a baby was born and the mother was bleeding, I injected her. When someone was suffering pain, I injected them; I did not only cause them to swallow medicine, I also knew how to inject medicine, causing some to swallow medicine, injecting others, even some little children. Doing that I lived here in Balta thinking, "Now it is good that I have started to be knowledgeable about medicines. Now I also know writing. I have not again lost my reading and writing. Now I can completely read writing. My ability to talk is good. Even though my outsider words are few, I am okay; I can speak them." For a long period of time my friend helped me each year by bringing medicines. Because of that he always made me work on my registers as he repeatedly came and went. When he had finished his other work he left me, going far away to his home village.

After Grompes started the official clinic in Balta, I acted only as an advisor and go-between, turning in his report forms at the regional hospital and getting medicines. When the clinic was first opened, people continued coming to our house in Balta, at all hours, as before, seeking medicines. To stop this, we took every bit of medicine we had in our house to the clinic and then got our medicine there, as everyone else did.

Grompes needed a lot of help with his paperwork, but as I remember, his forms were not filled out any more poorly than those of the other Health Promoters, both indigenous and mestizo. The problem was that Grompes was invisible to the officials at the hospital. They did not have the funds to supervise him in such an isolated location and he did not have the money nor desire to fly to Pucallpa, except with me. He was nonetheless almost removed from the Health Promoter roster in about 1976, when the director of the hospital began requiring that each Promoter have or obtain a secondary school diploma, in order to upgrade the position of Health Promoter. Grompes was truly a "barefoot doctor" and not even on the horizon to meeting such a requirement. But I had followed Professor Tapia's original advice, maintaining a speaking acquaintance with the hospital director. I went to him to plead Grompes' case, pointing out that I had heard him admonish his other Health Promoters by saying, "If Grompes, out on the Purús, without any formal education, can fill out these forms, you all, who have had primary school, can do it also." That was the argument that persuaded him to give Grompes a permanent position.

By 1972 Balta had a school and a clinic; we were on our way to functioning only as advisors. The Cashinahua were beginning to get the idea that they could handle these outside things themselves. With these two services and the beginnings of a village store in Balta, more and more families were moving there. Pudicho tells it this way.

> 67. At the same time my other child, my nephew [Mario] read what our parent God and our older brother Jesus had written long ago. He continued to read all that others had reported and he said to us, "Let's have our people live together. Let's dwell with our people. Let's invite our people to come here." He then invited them all to live here. He invited them from upriver; he invited them from the other rivers [in Brazil]; he invited them from downriver; he made them gather to him here over a period of many months.

When the group of 150 people arrived from the Jordan River in Brazil in 1973 they said that they had heard that people over here were not dying. That was true, since modern medicines were consistently available, very few babies and no elderly people had died.

Mario also describes that early period as follows.

> Then later at the time when Professor Tapia was making selections for named positions, you spoke to him on my behalf. And even though I did not know anything yet, he said to

you, "I can do it for you. I can assign a school and a teaching position to his community." By doing that he named me as an official teacher even though I did not have a complete set of personal documents.

However, even though it was something crucial and important, you suffered difficulties for me and helped me to get all my documents, my supplemental birth certificate, my military service card, my voter registration card, and a tax registration card. Even though I, by myself, did not get them, you, even you by helping me greatly, you were obtaining all my documents. Even though I was completely oblivious to when I was born, some outsider said, "Pick any date! It is not important." So I myself chose, I picked a date for you. And listening to us, they finished the documents long ago. After you did that, you packaged these government things and sent them to someone. Then after some months passed they officially contracted me to teach. Before this you paid me long ago. You were always saying, "As I tell you lots of different things, teach your people." In this way, you made me teach my people at each house without thinking of a school building at that time. You said to me, "Teach them. I will pay you what I can. I will help you." And then because I was teaching them, Professor Tapia named me to be a teacher.

Then my people made a separate school building for me, one set aside for that purpose. After they made the school building and left, my thinking was clear and good at that time. I thought, "As they are telling me, I cannot just teach a few. I will gather the entire population together. I intend to say, 'Come' to the entire population." I thought that and called everybody who had children to come. From downriver, from upriver, I gathered them to this village [Balta]. I started teaching lots of children, 105 little children, thinking to myself, "You are not able to teach that number of little children." I was also teaching various teenage women and teenage men while also taking on lots of other work; I was a teacher, a merchant, and teacher of the Gospel; also I was the one who had the medicines; you assigned all this work to me.

Professor Tapia wanted to see whether the teacher candidates and the sponsoring linguists were serious about having a school before he assigned positions. Mario was an enthusiastic student, and I was a persistent linguist, so after Mario had demonstrated his desire and ability by teaching three years at very low pay, an official school position was assigned to Balta. This was the start of a successful school program among the Cashinahua.

The Europeanized method of instruction, with students sitting before a teacher who was managing the instructional session, was completely foreign to the Cashinahua. So when Mario and Tomas started teaching, they had no experience of a well-managed classroom. In their classes at the government school at Yarinacocha, the professors were trying to teach them to use a globalization approach, i.e., a method where separate subjects—arithmetic, language, geography, etc.—are integrated. The professors, however, were not using the method they wanted the indigenous teachers to learn. They were using the old-fashioned lecture method, by which they had learned years before, to teach the newer method. Thus, Mario and Tomas had a difficult time discerning what was wanted. Fortunately, as they taught, their students grew up with classroom experience, so that when some of them later studied to become teacher candidates they were able to learn more easily.

Mario was the first Cashinahua in Peru to obtain all his personal documents. Even though his supplementary birth certificate came through painlessly, the other documents took much longer and required many more visits to various offices. The most difficult was the military service card. This was processed through the army, and we were requesting a waiver of military service for Mario because he was over age and a grandfather. Mario told me in 1994 about one visit to an office where I was talking enthusiastically to a captain or major who was not very sure about the North American speaking to him nor about the recent birth certificate being presented to him. But many smiles, patience, and an explanation of Mario's situation eventually secured the military service card. The most embarrassing visit was the one to the Registry of Elections office. The Registrar was Dini Fulano, who had been the first full-time river trader with the Cashinahua in Peru. He ushered Mario and me past all the other waiting people, treating Mario as a long lost relative. This preferential treatment was repeated each time I later took other Cashinahua men to the same office; fortunately, they all passed the written exam in Spanish.

Mario began to complain about the amount of work he thought I had assigned to him. By 1994 he had forgotten that he wanted to be a teacher and wanted to have Gospel meetings. Also, he was the one who heard from other teacher candidates that we could get a loan to buy things to start a village store. In 1971, Mario was the only one I knew who could handle the sale of things. But he was right, he was very busy being the first

Cashinahua in Peru to take on a paid specialization and not be just a hunter and horticulturist.[12]

Mario continues, telling how we resolved his problem.

> Then because I was not able to do that amount of work, you thought kindly toward me long ago. I said to you, "I am not able to do this amount of work. Because I continually teach and sell things, I am not able to teach afternoons."
>
> Then because I had spoken this to you, you said, "Okay, we can choose another." After we thought around the village as to which man we could choose, you said, "Which good man do you always observe?"
>
> I responded, "I myself observe Marcelino. We always see that Marcelino is a characteristically good man. He can do it. He can take care of the merchandise very well. Because he is like that, let's divide off the merchandise work to him," and we divided the work to him long ago.

Marcelino was a good choice because of his precision and straightforwardness. Even better, he was Grompes' cross-cousin and married to his sister, Alicia, Pudicho's only surviving daughter. This put him close to the leadership. Further, he had three brothers living in the village who would be supportive if necessary.

The main functions of the village store was to help the Cashinahua to obtain commercial goods, to demonstrate that they could manage their own affairs, and to provide a bit of competition to the river traders. There was very little cash money in Balta—only what we brought in to buy vegetables and meat, with the purpose of teaching the people to understand cash and how to count it. The traders did not use cash since they had their capital tied up in trade goods, outstanding debts, and skins or rubber. So the store had to join the system. But there was one strict rule—nothing was given on credit. This meant that Marcelino had to be firm with all his relatives, which was virtually everybody. This was a departure from their norm of sharing, though he would have shared the merchandise had it been his to share, but he consistently maintained that it was not his. Grompes and I supported him, and people soon grew accustomed to the idea, even his wife. Over the years the amount of available cash increased, but mostly Marcelino took credit slips. Grompes was the village

---

[12]Mario worked in his gardens and hunted on weekends and avoided paying anyone to do his garden work or hunt for him. He had cash from his teaching position to buy what he wanted without becoming indebted to a river trader. When Mario started teaching, the other men were gaining a lot more from skin hunting than he earned as a teacher. The market for skins disappeared, however, and he now has a retirement pension.

purchasing agent. He worked out of the various clinic buildings they built, and purchased artifacts—hammocks, woven bags, headdresses, carved wooden dolls, some clay things, and many bows and arrows. He gave the people credit slips, deducting the amount they owed for medicines. The people then took the credit slips to the store to exchange them for what they wanted. Grompes kept the artifacts at the clinic to be sent to Yarinacocha when there was room on an airplane. We then sold the artifacts or arranged for their sale and acted as wholesale buyers when we were at Yarinacocha.

Since no credit was extended, we devised an equitable scheme for the women who wanted to save for a large aluminum pot. If a woman had credit slips for half the price of the pot, Marcelino would write her name on the pot with a magic marker and put the credit slips inside, taping the lid shut. Then the woman added credit slips and claimed her pot when it was fully paid for—a sort of lay-away plan. The store was open only part time and was securely locked up when Marcelino went off to carry out his normal activities, or for months at a time when he went with us to Yarinacocha. I never heard that anything was stolen. The Cashinahua do not usually steal things from each other. Their society is so close and open that a theft would be difficult to hide.

Even though they lived in geographic isolation, I felt that I needed to help the Cashinahua prepare for the increasing contact with the outside world. This process of acculturation had been in motion in both directions since rubber tappers first contacted their parents and grandparents in Brazil. During that time the outsiders always told them what they wanted them to know, and the Cashinahua have learned to mistrust words that were not backed by actions. In their own culture they demonstrate what they want someone to learn. Therefore, I could not simply say that I was concerned for their welfare, I had to demonstrate it and show them what I wanted them to learn.

Pudicho is nearing the end of his narrative and now tells what it was like for him to again live in a large group after many families had moved to Balta.

> 68. While I dwelt with them, they produced lots of children, not just a few. They fathered many babies, both male children and female children. The grown teenage men were going about doing their normal activities while eyeing the teenage women who were their possible wives. The teenage women were going about doing their normal activities while evaluating the young men who were their possible husbands. And the recently-stood-up-ones [toddlers] were going around

with their parents visiting other houses. And the fast-growing ones were everywhere playing in the village. The adults again had lots of children, whom they made go about visiting their relatives, as we lived here across from the mouth of the side stream named Balta, where I dwell taking care of the airplane field.

He is saying that this is the way they lived before the activities of the outsiders scattered his people, and the epidemics of their sicknesses reduced their numbers. They had large settlements at the headwaters of the Curanja River before the majority of them went back to Brazil. Then by 1975 there were again enough young women and young men of the correct cross-cousin relationships to marry within the village; the young men did not have to leave to find an acceptable household. The young men were learning to work and hunt to make themselves acceptable as move-in husbands. The young women worked at home and went to the gardens with their mothers but did not become serious about learning their domestic skills until they had husbands to care for.

When we arrived in 1969, there were only a few newly married couples because there were very few young adults between the ages of 13 and 20 and more women than men. Most of the babies had died during the years prior to the coming of Ken Kensinger—the period when they had the repeated waves of outsider sicknesses.

Marriage exists as a means to invest their efforts in their children, especially daughters, in order to have someone to care for them in their old age. The women who were considered the most successful were those who had married daughters with sons-in-law contributing to the joint economic household. Most of the successful women we knew were co-wives in a polygynous relationship with a good hunter or a man who had been a good hunter. The best men were rewarded with two or even three wives, usually sisters or parallel cousin "sisters".

There are two ways that polygynous marriages are established. First, if a young man moves into his uncle's household on a tenuous marriage basis and turns out to be a good hunter and worker, he will be offered a second daughter when the first daughter bears her first child. Women try to avoid sexual intercourse for at least one year while nursing the baby. By offering the second daughter, the parents prevent the young man from seeking another household with an available daughter. In the early years of marriage a young man may be "thrown away" or leave of his own volition. So if the good hunter likes the household and other daughter, and she agrees, he stays and the sisters eventually cooperate in running a successful household, while taking care of their parents as they age. This arrangement has benefits for the young man, leaving him free to go on long hunts and further enhance his reputation. He does, however, have to eventually hunt more and cut a new garden, usually side by side, for each wife each year.

Second, an older man may gain an additional wife through several circumstances. If a brother dies he might inherit the widow and her children. Also a wife may want/need help running a busy household and say, "What, me do all the work? Go get another wife!" She may even already have someone in mind with whom she can get along. Also, women beyond their teen years may leave their parental home and join a successful man's household even though her parents may not like it because they do not get the benefit of a live-in working son-in-law.

In one situation two full sisters had been married to the same man for many years when a friend of theirs without any daughters was widowed. They did not want their friend to leave and move in with her dead husband's brother in another village, so they requested their husband to take her on as a wife, thus providing her with daughters to care for her in her old age. He did not want the extra work and responsibility of another wife, but they would not sleep with him nor feed him until he acquiesced. Now she has a married daughter and grandchildren.

Even though their marriage system has shown itself to be very successful for them, the outside world is forcing its viewpoint on their culture without understanding how practical and responsible the Cashinahua have been in the past concerning this family arrangement.

Pudicho continues by telling that when they were in contact with outsiders, while he was a young child, all his close relatives, ones we call "blood relatives" (aunts, uncles and cousins), died before his younger brothers were born. This indicates that there was a higher than normal death rate, even at that time.

> 69. My close relatives had died long ago; after my father had created only me, all my other close relatives died. The only close relatives I have are my brothers, and while I was living in this village with them, others of my people kept coming to join me. "Because we are interested in our older brother's words, let's live together with him. He is calling us," they said and kept coming to me over a period of many months. They built many houses and settled down.

The actual brothers he refers to are Idiodoro and Belisario. Incidentally, Pudicho demonstrates the male centeredness of his narrative by not mentioning a full sister, Louisa, wife of Araguana and mother of Mario.

The Cashinahua are quite aware of the difference between close relatives of varying degrees and classificatory relatives whose relationship is only known by their Genuine names. Idiodoro and Belisario addressed and referred to Pudicho as "older brother" because he was truly that. Others would do the same because he was older and was of the same namesake group. The word translated "older brother" also means "paternal grandfather". It is used in two ways—for the actual relationship as well as for a person in the same "namesake" group who is old enough to be one's grandfather (see Kensinger 1995:110, 166–167). Even though the men who were moving to Balta were referring to Pudicho as the one who was calling them, his son Grompes was the active village headman.

> 70. After they settled down, they made gardens and were eating from them; they dug cassava and were eating it; they collected bananas and were drinking banana gruel; they shot game animals and were eating the meat; while my people were doing all of this, I was living with them, I and my close relatives.

This period of high population at Balta was very difficult for Grompes because there were three or four former headmen who had come with their people and did not necessarily like having someone else be the village leader. In addition, the newcomers had to eat until their new gardens began to produce, which meant that Grompes, as Place Parent, had to coordinate the food sharing. No one challenged Grompes' position but the housing pattern developed into extended family neighborhoods with the newly-arrived headmen's houses as their centers.

The Cashinahua pride themselves on sharing with relatives, and a strong insult is to be called *Yauxi* 'miserly'. Usually, people may eat from their relatives' gardens with permission, but occasionally during that high population period the concept of permission was stretched. The provision of garden food to the newly arrived fell the hardest on Grompes because he was the headman who had to be the most generous and because he had three wives for each of whom he had to cut a new garden each year. One year during that time, as he was taking me for a tour of his new gardens, we came across some women harvesting cooking bananas in an old garden. After he spoke with them amiably, he said to me in a low voice as we headed on down the trail, "They didn't ask our wives' permission to harvest those bananas." (He said "our wives" because his wives are my classificatory cross-cousins, the same term as "wife".) As the gardens belonged individually to his wives, the owner should have been asked, even though that older garden was then producing only bananas.

Accelerated Change

I once asked one of the vigorous middle-aged men (20–40) how they provided for the less fortunate families and those of the few lazy men. He said that they planted extra large gardens and the women arranged it among themselves. Those sharing activities were not as obvious as the distribution of meat. When a man brings in meat, he gives it to his mother or his wife and she divides it among the close relatives. I have seen a man's sister walk over to his wife, who was cutting up a peccary, hold out her hand and say, "Mine." She was given a front leg. If it had been a less close relative, she may have gotten only a piece of backbone to add a little flavor to their boiled cassava root. We eventually learned that even though the men seem to be in charge, it is the women who keep the regular life of the community operating by means of their extended network of relatives and friends.

Pudicho now concludes his long narrative by saying that his people are finally returning to the good times, which in his mind existed before the privation caused by the original coming of the outsiders.

> 71. This generation of children is doing somewhat like it is reported that our ancient ones used to do when they had newly contacted the outsiders long ago. They have lived in this way and we are settled here; at the mouth of this side stream Balta we have lived in this way [1975].

Pudicho had other reasons to be satisfied at this time in his life. He had been repeatedly treated for intestinal parasites and amoeba and was feeling physically better than he had in over five years. Also, a younger woman had moved in with him for a few months and became pregnant before his relatives talked her into returning to her lazy husband. Grompes' wives told me that they had promised her that they would make sure the child had clothing in the future. This seems to be a present-day requirement of a father, even if he is separated from the mother.

Pudicho remained relatively active for an older man, cutting garden and going fish drugging, until 1979 when his liver failed, a common result of lifelong infestations of amoeba. He slowly grew weaker and jaundiced, as he had been when we first met him in 1969. When he finally slipped into a coma and died, the entire village, who had been slowly gathering, began to wail and cry, much as Pudicho told in chapter 4. They wailed and cried all night, singing the "send-the-spirit-away" song. In the morning the men wrapped his body in cloth and pieces of an old dugout canoe for burial. After his personal belongings were destroyed, the men of the other moiety took the body several hundred yards upstream and buried it among other graves without ceremony. In his case one exception was made. After a lengthy discussion about saving a large wooden storage chest his grandson Herman had made for him after he had studied carpentry at the government school at Yarinacocha, they finally decided to save it.

This was a concession to a new era when some things were not personally made by the deceased and were thus less attached to the person's spirit. After his body was buried, there was no extended lamenting, and life returned to an appearance of normality. However, on the following day and for about five days thereafter, the older men gathered at Pudicho's house to chant and dance the *Chidin*. They took turns wearing Pudicho's harpy eagle feather and macaw tail-feather ceremonial costume. With one man on each side of the costumed man, facing backwards, they shuffled up and down the palm bark floor of Pudicho's house chanting the *Chidin*. Grompes explained to me that this was to aid his father's spirit's journey to the Ancient Ones. The Cashinahua believe that the spirit of a man with much knowledge and power is challenged by powerful spirits. By doing the *Chidin*, the men were aiding Pudicho's spirit to overcome those challenges.

Pudicho was considered a successful person. He had brought his group to a place where they could get the things he had always wanted for them—cloth and metal pots for the women and metal tools and guns for the men. His son, Grompes, had a permanent position as a Health Promoter; his sister's son, Mario, was a government bilingual schoolteacher; and many of his grandchildren, including Grompes' daughter Juana, would also become bilingual schoolteachers. But more important for him was the fact that his only living daughter, Alicia, remained faithful to him until he died, seeing to it that he was fed and clothed, just as she had done for her mother. I hope that this feature of their culture never changes. However, change does continue and in the next chapter both Mario and Grompes tell about further developments that affect their lives.

10

The Present-Day Situation

By the time we left Peru in 1981, there were five officially appointed schoolteachers, teaching in three schools: two at Balta, one at Santa Rey (just upstream from Balta), and two at Conta (on the Purús River near Esperanza). Not only had the teachers mastered their school lessons, they had also mastered the rosters and report forms of the Peruvian national school system. When they had begun teaching in the early 1970s, I needed to help them quite often with their paperwork. By 1977, however, knowing we would be finishing our linguistic project and translation work in four or five years, I had to assure that they would stop depending on me for help. So I told them that they had to make friends at the regional Ministry of Education office in Pucallpa and find someone to help them make the final corrections on their rosters and forms. This was the same advice Professor Tapia had given me many years before. They understood very well, because they knew that many other teachers had someone check over their forms before they were turned in. What they did not like, however, was paying the "friend" to check their forms. Although this method was definitely outside their cultural norms, they needed to learn to function on their own within the Peruvian norms, and they did. I think this change also caused them to be more conscious of their accuracy throughout the school year (April through December).

Previously, the Cashinahua had seen reading and writing as outsider concepts and were always mystified by the outsiders' use of accounts, documents, and forms. They had grown up in a face-to-face society, displaying their intelligence by being able to gain a living from the very complex rain forest. In fact, their traditional ways had no need of reading and writing; they memorized what they needed to know and sent messages by word of mouth. In the mid-1940s, however, they made the choice to contact and work with the Peruvian outsiders, which eventually meant being able to function in both worlds. The teachers, who presently number fifteen (1994), have handled the adaptation best, because they were obliged to interface with the outside world when they attended school near Pucallpa every January through March to continue their own education. But Grompes required less contact and has had more difficulty. He tells it as follows.

> After he left, I stayed settled, treating with medicine whatever pains my people were suffering. Then the hospital leaders called me a second time, saying, "Bring the same written documents you got long ago. Bring your entrance documents and proof of the year you graduated."
>
> I tried to go but the Instituto leader Jaime [Daggett] prohibited me, saying, "Don't come. Have someone bring the documents to me. Send to me whatever written documents you have, but don't come. Whatever they wrote for you when you entered the medical course and whatever certificates they gave you when you finished the course, give them all to me." I gave him all of my papers. Being interested in me, Jaime went to talk about me with the outsiders.
>
> And the director said, "He certainly does not qualify. We must throw him off the list."
>
> Then Jaime responded, "He should not be thrown off the list. He is a grown man. His friend Ricardo likes him very much. His friend speaks his words. His friend is a powerful person. By means of powerful words he is causing him to learn. Because of that he passed his course work. He is a grown man, not a youth." Saying this, he spoke to the outsider boss, not the leader of a village but he spoke that to the chief doctors at the hospital.
>
> Then one of them said, "If that is the situation, everything is okay. I believe you," and they stopped trying to throw me off the roster of Health Promoters. After they left me alone and had finally given me the various forms to fill out each month, I wrote them out for them each month and sent then to the hospital. Then I left off doing it temporarily. I left off doing the forms for one year; then Joy arrived at my village. My teacher, the nurse Joy, arrived and asked, "How goes it? Where are your registers?"

The Present-Day Situation

> I answered, "I don't have any."
> She said, "Don't you ever do them? You must do them."
> I said, "Okay. Give me some."
> She gave me some registers, saying, "Do them always like this," and she herself did some for me.
> I said, "Okay," and after she again left, I did the registers. My friend Ricardo's people, who are very very knowledgeable about medicines, caused all things to come out well for me long ago.
> Now I always do these things, "Look here."

I felt disappointed to hear this because I had worked with Grompes more than with the teachers. I had always helped him in the clinic and checked his rosters and report forms when I was in Balta. But because I had acted as his go-between with the hospital in Pucallpa, he had never developed the concept of relating directly to a bureaucracy, as did the teachers. During those years, transportation to and from the Purús region was mostly by expensive charter flights and as he said, he did not have money to travel to Pucallpa. I am also sure that the nurse, Joy Congdon, who was part of the staff who trained him, made a supervisory visit to Balta almost every year up until we left in 1981. However, during those years the report forms would have looked good to her because I had been helping him, as a Genuine brother should have done.

I do not remember being told about the time Jim Daggett had to intercede for Grompes at the hospital. During the 1980s I made visits to Balta every other year. This was probably what Grompes was referring to when he said that Jim Daggett told the hospital directors that I was still helping him. I made those visits to continue my relationships and language ability with the Cashinahua. I now realize that many aspects of culture can be learned only through long-term exposure. Grompes, Mario, and Marcelino continue to write letters and notes to me but they seldom give me enough contextual information to be able to fully understand the situations they are writing about. Many of them still have a face-to-face mentality, assuming that the person to whom they are writing is still living within the context that makes their utterances comprehensible.

Grompes now tells of another frustration, also shared by the teachers.

> However, when my authorization documents first came out long ago, they asked me, "When your money comes, where and how shall we handle it?"
> I said, "I do not know. I do not know how to store money. I do not know the authorized agent of the teachers. I do not know the name of an agent."

Then they also got an authorized agent for me, saying, "We intend to have Victor act as agent for you." After they assigned Victor to be my proxy to collect my pay, he sent me only a small amount of money each month. Finally, I learned of the percentage he was keeping and said, "That is bad. He is stealing from me." Changing to another agent, I threw Victor away. To Manuel, his surname I have forgotten, Manuel whatever, to him I changed. Then he was sending me money; after he had been sending money for several months, I looked at my account with him; he was only giving me a very small amount. Then I threw him away also, and thought, "Whom may I choose? Okay, I intend to choose Miguel," and I asked Miguel [a store keeper in Esperanza].

At first he said, "I cannot do it for you," but later he said to me, "Truly, you like me. I can do it for you." He said this several years ago.

The need to have someone with the power of attorney to receive the pay of someone working for the government in an isolated location has been a recurring problem for a long time in Peru. It is even more difficult for indigenous people, who have no relatives they can trust in the city or town where the pay must be collected. In Peru, paychecks for teachers and health promoters are issued each month and must be picked up within a month or be returned to Lima. So each teacher or health promoter who cannot get there, must have an "empowered" person to collect the check at the appropriate Ministry office. It can then be cashed only at the government bank, the Bank of the Nation. This person must be a Peruvian citizen with personal documents. As foreign advisors, we were not permitted to be involved, except as messengers after the cash was obtained.

Grompes has been a health promoter for over twenty years, and I remember that Victor was his first authorized agent and did not take more than the legally allowed percentage. As I recall it was between 25 and 30 percent. This amount seemed high to Grompes, because his monthly wage was equivalent to only about fifty U.S. dollars, and he was not accustomed to the normal Peruvian business markups. Also, Grompes is again telescoping the past in his narrative, covering almost twenty years as if it were only a few. Like Grompes, most of the Cashinahua schoolteachers have found it convenient to have merchants in Puerto Esperanza as their authorized agents, because they travel to Pucallpa each month and can pick up and cash their checks for them. I do not know if these agents charge a fee, but I do know that the teachers and Grompes carry accounts with these merchants. If the patrón or agent is honest and caring, they are satisfied to have that outsider handle business deals with the larger world of Peru for them.

Grompes continues by telling of his more recent problems with the bureaucracy.

> And now I always work with him, but various doctors come to Puerto Esperanza and then go home. They always change where they live and go home and then another one comes and calls me to come to Pucallpa.
>
> Each time I told them, "I cannot go because I am without money."
>
> However, they were always writing, "No, it cannot be that way. Come!" Again another doctor came to Esperanza and wrote to me, "Okay, even though you have learned about medicine, you never go to Pucallpa. Gifts and things always come for you and when you never come to get them, someone always takes them on you." Each doctor did this and then went home. Then another doctor came here to Balta by canoe and said to me, "Grompes, why don't you go to Pucallpa? Medicines and other gifts for you are in the refrigerated storeroom at the hospital. You have a motor to go downriver with. Even though there are things at the hospital for you, you always lose out on them. Can you go with me?"
>
> I said, "I can go."
>
> Then the doctor said, "Okay, at other times in the past I have always sent you lots of clothing. Do you get them?"
>
> I answered, "I never get them."
>
> And he said, "That is bad. They are stealing from you in Esperanza. You yourself, go to Pucallpa!" I listened to him and went with him to Esperanza but I was frustrated in going because I was timid and did not have confidence to travel to Pucallpa on the government airplane. I stayed there in Esperanza for a month or so and finally came back here to Balta.
>
> Then, when last year was ending, at the time when the year was going away, I again went to Esperanza, and a woman said to me, "Come here right away. Do you have Social Insurance? Do you have your insurance card?"
>
> So I said, "I have."
>
> She said, "Good. Sign this for me."
>
> I went into her boss's office and he said, "You are not on the list. Where is your Social Insurance Card?"

I said, "This is it," showing him my other personal identification cards.

The man said, "You don't have an Insurance Card. They must have thrown you off the list a few years ago."

Then a young woman said, "He is not thrown off the list. He is a regular. He works as a Medical Auxiliary; the state always pays him. He is now a regular. Thus we cannot throw him off the list." Finally, he understood and left me alone. Because of that I am settled here in Balta continually doing my work. I am not afraid of them.

Grompes is revealing how reticent he was to increase his direct contacts with the regional hospital and the doctors who are periodically assigned to the clinic in Puerto Esperanza. Peru requires that all new doctors serve a period of government service. Since the Purús region is one of the more isolated areas, there is not a continuity of personnel. As long as I was in Peru, Grompes was content to have me as a go-between. In his thinking, it was the same as having a river trader as a go-between to obtain the things he wanted. Unlike the teachers, he was not required nor paid enough to regularly travel to Pucallpa. Also Grompes knew that the government air service to the Purús region was irregular, depending on the weather and the attitude of the military pilots who were stationed in Lima. The pilots had good reason to be leery because one of their military cargo planes crashed in 1979 while trying to find Puerto Esperanza during cloudy weather. This has changed somewhat with the use of better navigation equipment and the paving of the previous 1,000-meter grass airstrip. In addition, Grompes had no friends or relatives to stay with if he did go to visit the hospital in Pucallpa. The teachers could stay at the housing provided at the Ministry of Education school at Yarinacocha. The Ministry of Health had no housing at the hospital compound because their other health promoters were all from the Ucayali River Valley and did not have to wait one to two weeks for an airplane to return home.

Theoretically, Grompes should be working with the government health clinic in Puerto Esperanza. In a letter (December 1996), however, he told me that since he was not part of their operation, he had to deal directly with the hospital in Pucallpa. There are no other paid indigenous health promoters in the Purús region of Peru, and the mestizo population is reticent to accept the indigenous people as full citizens even if they have the required personal documents. This is partly due to an ongoing attitude that indigenous people are minors and must be taken care of by the state.

The state health service was very good at providing various vaccines during the time we were in Peru, and recently they have been sending vaccination teams by river from Puerto Esperanza to visit all the indigenous villages. But since Grompes was trained and appointed in 1972, there has been no move to have paid health promoters in the other indigenous villages. This may be one of the reasons why many of the Cashinahua have moved downriver to be within easy river travel of Puerto Esperanza and its services. I hope that with improved air service, Grompes can relate better to his supervisors at the hospital in Pucallpa and work out some arrangement that will satisfy all the parties.

In 1994 I learned that the indigenous schoolteachers are taking advantage of the improved transportation situation. Previously, they used more expensive charter flights to come in for their continuing education and then to return in time to start teaching in their schools by the first of April. Now they can travel to Puerto Esperanza by canoe and be relatively sure of flights that will get them to and from Pucallpa in time for their classes. In 1994 the teachers in Balta and Santa Rey were even able to tell me which stores in Pucallpa had the items they asked me to buy after I returned there.

The bilingual schools in the Cashinahua villages have been a success in making a vast majority of the young adults literate in their own language. Also, most of the men thirty-five and under are enabled to become literate in Spanish, depending on how long they stayed in school. Most of the young women have had only three or four years of primary school because they start school later than the boys and are usually married at age 12 or 13, at which time they must work more at home with their mothers. The older women have never been enthusiastic about their daughters going to school because they fear schooling will induce their daughters to abandon them in their old age. As far as I know this has not occurred and the mothers continue to instill in their daughters the obligation to stay with them.

Grompes' wives have all their daughters living with them in Balta. I was sorry, however, to learn recently (February 1997) that Ana's only daughter Juliana has died, leaving several young children (this is the Ana who told of losing all her children and husband in the early epidemics.) This leaves Ana in a precarious situation because daughters are the primary caregivers for aged women. She has two sons living in Balta who I hope will care for her. However, past examples that we have seen do not offer much hope because sons are socialized to bond to their wives' families. The best outcome would be for Ana's "son-in-law" (the father of her grandchildren) to marry a woman who is already Ana's classificatory daughter, meaning the new wife would already be an "other mother" to the children. I hope Grompes does something to demonstrate familial concern for his aged wife. As I remember, Grompes' youngest wife is relatively friendly with Ana.

On a lighter note, Grompes' daughter Juana, his second oldest daughter with his longest-term wife, Maria, continued in school when the other girls her age quit and has herself become a schoolteacher. She is married to another schoolteacher and had her eighth child in 1995 while still teaching. Her mother, Maria, who lives with them, is a great help with her grandchildren and has secured a well-earned old age situation, even though she is only about sixty years old and still in good health.

In 1994 I asked Grompes how many grandchildren he had and he said he did not know; concern for exact numbers is an outsider concept. Grompes was content to know that his grandchildren were living near him. He was, however, willing to indulge my question. I knew that he had eleven children who survived to have children. So we added up the number of children each had, coming to a total of fifty-seven. He then told me that three of his grandchildren had one child each. By now, I expect that there are more children in each category.

In 1994 the Cashinahua population in Peru had reached about 1,300 and is definitely increasing. Their increase is both intentional and the result of changing circumstances. I agree with Kensinger when he says that the Cashinahua see the increase in the number of children as a guarantee of their survival as a society (1995:271). The Cashinahua have always been proud of their children. Many times the maternal grandparents are more proud than the young parents, leading me to believe that grandchildren are a mark of reproductive success and hope for a contented old age.

I do not feel that there are more pregnancies than in previous years. The Cashinahua women habitually nurse their children up to three years, and the contraceptive effect of lactating may or may not delay the next pregnancy. In the past, if a woman became pregnant too soon after the normal one year of refraining from sexual contact after the birth of a baby, and she felt that her nursing child would not survive leaving the breast, she would abort the new baby. This was part of their strategy to nurture as many children as possible to a productive adulthood. At this time, however, because the women are in better health and are more assured of a consistent supply of food and medicines than in the past, I believe they are not aborting as many of the first postpartum pregnancies as before. The women may also be subconsciously influenced by the general desire of the men to increase their numbers to obtain a more secure political position in the mixed society of the Alto Purús region.

Their changing attitudes in addition to the declining infant death rate have produced an increased population. This is not yet a threat to the carrying capacity of the area of Peru in which they live. On the other hand, a limiting factor for the Cashinahua is the quantity of salable goods and services they need to produce and exchange with the outside world in order to get the things they now feel they need. Working logs and rubber was what first drew them down to live by the navigable water, and later they had a "golden age" when skin hunting utilized their special skills. Sending logs downriver has continued to provide a small amount of income, but Peru limits this by wanting the logs sawn before the wood goes on to Brazil.

Beginning in the early 1980s the authorities in Puerto Esperanza have tried to develop their region by introducing cattle to most of the indigenous villages. This has been only marginally successful because the transportation of a live full-grown cow or bull by dugout canoe is difficult and the price paid for the cattle is low. Puerto Esperanza is the only market and the officials set the price schedule to their own advantage for whatever people in their town buy from the indigenous people.

In 1994 the Purús region was again experiencing good economic times because of generous government subsidies from Lima. Under President Fujimori's leadership, the government had designated the Purús region a "frontier zone" which meant it receives extra funds for infrastructural development. The largest projects that have affected the indigenous people are the extension and paving of the airstrip, the provision of regular subsidized air service from and to Pucallpa using Peruvian air force cargo planes, and an aggressive school construction program. As mentioned earlier, the improved air service greatly helps the Cashinahua schoolteachers travel to Pucallpa for their continuing education and necessary visits to the Ministry of Education regional headquarters. And the new school buildings are better than the dirt-floored, thatch-roofed schools they previously built themselves.

The moneys that enter the Purús region via pay for the army, police, civil servants, construction workers, schoolteachers, and health workers are all government funds. These funds produce some internal commerce and a market for the meat and garden crops the indigenous people can deliver to Puerto Esperanza. This gives them the opportunity to buy necessities such as ammunition, pots, kerosene, gasoline, matches, cloth, clothing, and the much-loved little glass beads. But the indigenous people are finding it very difficult to replace the sewing machines, shotguns, and motors they obtained during the golden age of skin hunting in the 1980s. The Purús region basically does not have a commodity to send out in exchange for what needs to be brought in.

Lima's present proprietary and paternalistic attitude toward the region may be influenced by Brazil's historic desire to acquire more of the Purús River's drainage. The northern portion of Peru's Purús province is a salient that reaches into Brazilian territory on both sides of the Purus River. I have seen on a map of the Brazilian province of Acre a proposed highway leading up to Peruvian territory on one side of the salient and then continuing on the other side, with the same route number on both sides. If it is built straight through it would pass close to Puerto Esperanza. This map was shown to me soon after the mestizo population of Puerto Esperanza sent a letter (about 1973) to the Brazilian capital requesting that their government take the territory because Peru was not giving them any services. It was soon after this that the Peruvian army established a base in Puerto Esperanza. An economic study of the Purús region would be an aid to understanding the present situation of the Cashinahua and the other indigenous groups who live there, but is beyond the scope of this study.

As he finishes his narrative, Mario Bardales tells of some of the more recent changes around him. He is not happy about these events nor about the diminished status of Balta since he was the one who actively invited the Cashinahua to congregate there.

> We continue to dwell here. They have forgotten how to be motor mechanics; not wanting to learn they have forgotten what they knew. They also ran the village store incorrectly; saying, "Who knows?" they finished it off and extinguished it.

The underlying attitude of the Cashinahua toward material things is to use them, wear them out, and then get others. This began when their ancestors made all that they used from what they found in the rain forest. This attitude has carried over to the things they obtain from the outside, including their invaluable shotguns. I could never get them to dry and oil their guns when they came in from the jungle. They did not see the Peruvians maintaining their shotguns. Neither did they see the outsiders maintaining and repairing their motors, so after they obtained motors to propel their canoes, they asked me to teach them how to care for them. I taught a few of them during the 1970s but did not have time to run a proper course. I then arranged for a mechanic friend to come to Balta and run a two-week motor course in 1979 or 1980. Some of the men learned to do standard maintenance and replace all the parts, except the crankshaft, on a 9 horse-power Briggs and Stratton engine. I think this is the group that Mario refers to. He may be correct concerning most of them, but on my visits during the 1980s and then again in 1994, they were keeping their motors running. They may have given up on some of the older motors because they could not get parts from the newer merchants in Puerto Esperanza.

After the skin hunting era ended, most of the river traders, such as Señor Gamboa, moved on or died. The one remaining river trading family, the Hoyles, are involved with trade downriver to and from Brazil. The newer merchants have not been river traders and have no need to travel the river to visit the various indigenous groups. This gives them a different perspective on the needs of the indigenous people and because of the low turnover they do not stock many motor parts. Most parts are purchased by the schoolteachers when they go to Pucallpa. An ordinary Cashinahua man who only hunts and makes gardens can no longer afford to buy a motor as Belisario and the others did during the time when they were permitted to hunt skins.

Even though economic conditions changed, Marcelino was able to keep the community store at Balta operating until the early 1990s by not extending credit. He had the backing of his cross-cousin, the headman Grompes, until there was a change in the village leadership. I was told that an indigenous man, a Shipibo from the Ucayali Valley, arrived with documents stating that he was an authorized government community development worker. He said he came to get the Cashinahua organized to better deal with the merchants in Puerto Esperanza. His first decision was that they should choose a different headman, a younger man who could speak better Spanish than Grompes. Their choice, Pepe's son Guillermo, a very intelligent and capable young man, could have been a good one. However, he also took over management of the village store and could not resist the pleas of his relatives, almost everybody, to extend them credit. By extending credit and not collecting what was owed he allowed to happen what Mario said, "They finished it off and extinguished it." Because of the culture, Guillermo could not insist that his close relatives pay, so no one else paid either. Marcelino, disturbed by the turn of events, went downriver to visit in Brazil with thoughts of getting backing to open another store. But no one wanted to back him because they did not think he was acculturated enough to pay the bribes that were necessary to pass the border posts.

In the meantime there was dissension in Balta, causing various groups to leave, as Mario told me.

> How I am living at this time, how I continually live, I am telling you. Listen carefully.
>
> At this time, even though I have not yet retired from teaching, I do not go to Yarinacocha to study anymore. Maybe they

have already terminated me? Even though I am waiting to see how things turn out with my retirement papers, I continue to live here and teach. I have made a certain quantity of little children grow up, as if it were yesterday. Have you seen the quantity of students that I have raised up?

Lots of children, whom I made grow up, are now teaching in various schools. Many students of the students whom I taught long ago, are downriver now. Some are teachers. Some are village leaders. Another one may have been a soldier. Another one studied to be an agricultural technician. Another is studying at the University in Pucallpa. Did he go there the other day?

Lots of my students are finishing their studies. Now they are changing into outsiders, with outsider names, with outsider words, and with outsider clothes. They are surpassing me and continually changing. Even though I myself taught them, I am now below them. They will all surpass me.

But it is true; you did everything for me long ago. You taught me long ago. As you did continually to me, I am continually doing to those who live in this village. When I was teaching them, this entire village was living well. Did I make them happy? Did I act as a merchant for them? Did I make their children grow up? By causing their children to learn and to play at school they were living happily here. Then after I graduated them, they themselves became teachers and wanted to live separately and continually went downriver. Because of that, many people, even though they had lived here, separated themselves completely from us, going away. Now the outsiders say that we only live in family groups. I myself and my leader [Grompes], and Eusebio also—Is it that number of families?—who live here now. These same ones, we are living here now. But at a faraway time, an uncountable number used to live here. Then many various ones, speaking bad of us, went away in groups. They, themselves, having done various bad things, wanted to separate from us. Separately, they themselves wanted to be village leaders. Wanting to be close to the outsiders, but still separate from them, they have settled at the edge of the outsiders' area in order to easily go and request things. They have completely gone away; only a few of us live here.

In early 1994 the District School Director in Puerto Esperanza told Mario that the government was changing the retirement law for teachers. If Mario did not apply for retirement status then, he would not be able to retire for many more years and then only with about half the amount of pay. Mario had more than the required twenty years of official service and applied for retirement. Later he wrote to me saying that his retirement had come through at the end of 1994.

But there is more to the story than simply helping Mario obtain just compensation for his years of service. The Ministry of Education has established secondary schools at Conta on the Purús River and at Balta on the Curanja River to serve the increasing number of Cashinahua young people finishing primary school and wishing to continue their education. The wife of the mestizo secondary school director in Balta told me that she wanted Mario to retire so she could take his place as director of the primary school, even though the original authorization for the school in Balta was for a bilingual school with a bilingual teacher. She does not speak Cashinahua, and Mario's assistant teacher, Jorge, would normally take over as the school's director. Jorge's current job as assistant would then be filled by one of the Cashinahua candidates who had studied at the teacher training course with the hope that there would be an opening someday. This situation seems to indicate that there is a movement to ease out the indigenous teachers and replace them with Spanish-speaking teachers who could not find positions in the Ucayali Valley.

When Mario spoke of his students surpassing him, he was being nostalgic and feeling sorry for himself. He grew up at the time his group was again making peaceful contact. He knows the old bow-and-arrow ways and took the lead in the new ways. He has done better financially than his cross-cousin Grompes but he is being surpassed by his own students who are academically superior to him. He was a grandfather when I began helping him through school and he had to adjust to the culturally different concept of functioning in a classroom. His students, however, have the advantage of growing up with a classroom experience and a better command of Spanish. Three of his students, who are now school directors, were tutored by me before they entered the teacher training course in Yarinacocha. I did not want them to have the same problems that Mario had.

The tendency to move ever closer to the source of supply has been the theme of Cashinahua history since the beginning of Pudicho's story. This desire is also noted by Schultz in his account of visiting the Cashinahua (chapter 6). Aside from those who moved downriver at the time of the disruption over leadership and the village store in Balta, various groups have continued to move downriver ever since the large increase of population at Balta in the early 1970s. The first group to move downriver contained most of the people who came from the Jordan River in Brazil (chapter 9). They had been more accustomed to close contact with Brazilian outsiders and did not like Grompes' prohibition of sugarcane rum, which was used by the river traders to entice clients. The only time I saw a fight between two Cashinahua men (normally they avoid coming to blows by avoidance or by moving away) was when they had been drinking white rum. Those from Brazil moved to Conta on the Purús River. They joined a group of Cashinahua who had come from the Embira River in Brazil and lived in Puerto Esperanza for a while. Later they moved upriver to Conta to avoid competition with the mestizos for garden sites and hunting territory near Puerto Esperanza.

The area around Balta could not sustain the horticultural and hunting needs of the five hundred or so inhabitants who attempted to live there in the early 1970s to take advantage of the new school and clinic. At first the men told me that they were willing to cut their gardens farther away than usual and travel an hour or so before they could start hunting, so that their children would stay alive and be able to go to school. This situation lasted until the late 1970s. At first the students from Santa Rey came to Balta each day, and the students from Curanjillo stayed with relatives in Balta during the school year. The second bilingual school was opened in Conta on the Purús River in about 1975. Soon after that there was an unofficial school in Santa Rey, which eventually received official status.

These were the four Cashinahua villages in Peru when we left in 1981, but even by then the reasons to stay at Balta were weakening. The last of the river traders, Herman and Alberto, who had learned to speak some Cashinahua, died in the 1979 cargo plane crash. The newer merchants no longer came to Balta because wild rubber and cat skins were no longer worth the trip and they took the peccary skins only if they were delivered to them. There were enough young men who had entered the government teacher training course as candidates to start unofficial schools and seek authorization and pay. So when their old houses at Balta needed to be rebuilt or rethatched, the heads of several extended families took that opportunity to move down toward the mouth of the Curanja River and on down the Purús River toward Puerto Esperanza. This gave them access to garden plots and hunting areas closer to their houses. The heads of extended families could again be headmen, living with their close relatives and the husbands of their daughters and granddaughters. This gave them the advantages of group living without the social pressures of a large village, though they still had enough people to continue cooperative labor when necessary.

As of 1994 there were thirteen Cashinahua villages in Peru: Santa Rey, Balta, Colombiano, Curanjillo, Nueva Luz, and Miguel Grau on the Curanja River; Libia, Cashuera, Bufeo, Canta Gallo, Pikiniki, Conta, and San Francisco on the Purús River. In all these villages the younger men are taking over leadership. Some of the older men whom we first met in 1969 are still alive but their sons, who have gone to school, are the new headmen. Before recontact with outsiders, the signs of leadership were the knowledge of ceremonies and the possession of a headman's harpy eagle and macaw feather ceremonial costume. Now, it is the possession of personal documents and the ability to deal successfully with the authorities in Puerto Esperanza to obtain official recognition and a land title for their community.

In 1977 the Cashinahua of the villages of Balta, Curanjillo, and Santa Rey on the Curanja River, and Conta on the Purús River had been given legal recognition by Peru and title to land around their villages. But this land was on only one side of the river, leaving them vulnerable to colonization and encroachment by mestizos at some future date. Furthermore, the amount of land was calculated only on the villagers' agricultural needs; it did not take into account the amount of territory needed for hunting. Hunting territory for the Cashinahua can be viewed as two-zoned—an area near the village which is hunted by use of private trails reaching out about one day's walk and more distant areas where hunting camps are set up. The latter may even require a canoe trip up or down the river. These less-hunted areas and even more distant hinterlands are necessary for the continued existence of some game animals, such as howler monkeys, deer, and peccary, to reproduce and increase their numbers before they migrate to within hunting range of the villages. The Cashinahua men told me that they try never to shoot the leader of a peccary herd. If they did, a new lead sow would not follow the previous circuit which passes near their village on their continual search for food. Previously, when they lived on the uplands away from the rivers, they moved their villages to new areas when game animals became scarce. But now that they have settled on the river's edge to remain in contact with their outside source of manufactured goods, they have had to change their hunting strategies.

In 1994 the need for larger tracts of land for the indigenous lifestyle was recognized by the authorities in Lima. All the established indigenous villages in the Purús region, including all thirteen Cashinahua villages, were given title to extended tracts of land. This was done through the efforts of the Asociación Interétnica de Desarrollo de la Selva Peruana with financing from the Danish government and much work by several European anthropologists. Concerning this new situation Kensinger wrote the following:

> Until the early 1990s villages fissioned when factions were unable to resolve their differences. One or more of the dissenting factions would move to a new site and establish a new village on unoccupied territory. However, all the land on both sides of the Purús River, from the Brazilian border to well above the mouth of the Curanja River and on both sides of the Curanja as far as Santa Rey, the village an hour upriver from Balta, is now vested in the inhabitants of each village and thus controlled by the headman and his faction. Dissenting factions will either have to convince the dominant faction of their village or the owners of another village to share part of their territory with them or they will have to move upriver, something they probably would be reluctant to do since the Peruvian town of Esperanza has become the most important, if not the only, source of goods, and proximity to it is considered highly desirable. (Kensinger 1998:29–32)

This recent acquisition of legal title to large tracts of land can definitely lead to significant cultural changes for the Cashinahua and the other indigenous groups. If Kensinger is correct, the headmen would become chiefs with coercive power over those who live in their villages' territory. For any indigenous group in the Purús region to make such a change, they would have to change their basic premise that land is to be used and then abandoned for another location.

The change from feet as the principal mode of locomotion to dugout canoes and then airplanes over the last fifty years certainly has challenged this premise, but I do not think it has fundamentally changed it. The Cashinahua still vote with their feet. Any extended family group will still move to any open section of river edge if they feel uncomfortable under the persuasive authority of any headman, giving no regard to outsiders' land papers. I also doubt that any headman and his faction would be allowed by the Peruvian authorities to resort to force if a new village were impinging on their active hunting zone or garden areas. The titles to the village territories are based on the "police powers" of the Peruvian state, but it would be unwise for the authorities to use these powers to enforce the word of village headmen who want to behave like a coercive chief. I think the realities of the rain forest environment will challenge and modify the use of those land grants. Manmade ideas and things are maintained only by continual attention.

Another reality affecting these land grants is the possibility of oil deep underground. The land was granted to the indigenous groups based on Royal law, not English Common law. This means that the people holding the title documents have only usufruct rights to the surface of their land. The government retains subsurface and access rights for roads, etc., with the need only to notify the usufruct holder of any change in the status of the land.

In the early 1970s, when there was a rush of oil exploration in the rain forest area of Peru, it was recognized that the rock formations under the Purús region had a good possibility of yielding oil and/or natural gas. The region's extreme isolation deterred further exploration. But in 1994 exploration crews had begun making use of the regular air link to Puerto Esperanza and were doing preliminary work near the Sharanahua village of Gasta Bala up the Purús River from the mouth of the Curanja River. If the suspected oil or gas is discovered in sufficient quantities, the government will eventually push a road from the Ucayali or Urabamba rivers out to the Purús region. When this happens, the Cashinahua and the other indigenous groups will lose the protection provided by geographic isolation. If a road comes, the Cashinahua will either have to compete with the Peruvian settlers who are certain to come or back away from the settlers and stay on the periphery of the development.

During the mid-1980s the Alto Purús area was upgraded by the government in Lima from a District to a Province, with Puerto Esperanza as the capital. This meant that all the indigenous people could obtain their personal documents there without having to travel to Pucallpa. Several young men have voluntarily entered the army, but the others were given military waivers so they could complete their personal documents. They told me that virtually all the men and some of the women who have finished primary school have completed their documentation. Traditionally, the women have seen their role as being in the village and its environs, leaving the external affairs to the men. Thus, they have sought less schooling and direct contacts with outsiders.

The interethnic raiding that was still happening in the 1930s and 40s stopped by the time the Cashinahua moved down to the Curanja River. Epidemics had reduced any population pressures that may have been a factor in past raiding. The increase in the police powers on both sides of the border have provided the present generations with a peaceful situation without worry that another ethnic group might push them off their land. However, in August 1994, a group of Cashinahua men who were going far up the Curanja River in search of turtle eggs, met the Mashku-Piro Indians for the first time. Since we arrived in 1969, the men had reported seeing footprints and temporary camps of someone hunting at the extreme headwaters of the Curanja River in the area where Pudicho's people hid after their escape from Brazil. The leader of the group who met these people lives in Santa Rey and tells of the encounter as follows.

I, Filomeno Torres, went about thinking the other day. While I was thinking, I said to my nephew Pedro, "It is good. They say that there are lots and lots of turtles crawling out on the beaches to lay eggs. Let's go get their eggs." After I said that to him, I said, "Good, wait while I ask about a canoe." I then asked to borrow my brother Tomás's canoe. I asked to borrow a small canoe and his daughter's husband ordered me to take it. That was good and I told Daniel, "I intend to go get turtle eggs. Let's all go get turtle eggs."

Then my grandson said to me, "Cross-cousin, take me!"

I answered, "Good. Let's go!"

Then my young son said, "I am going also."

And I sighed, "Okay. Let's all go as a group."

Then at 8 o'clock in the dark we left the other day. Going in the dark; by means of a flashlight we went and cut four stalks of cooking bananas. After, I cut them, we loaded them into the canoe and continued. Then we nosed the canoe into the riverbank at my son's garden and dug up six clusters of cassava. After I knocked all the dirt off the cassava tubers, I loaded them into the canoe. Then we slept at that same place and after I awoke the next morning, I went down to the beach and found two nests where turtles had laid their eggs. Out of one I got eighteen eggs, out of the other I got twenty eggs.

Then I said, "Let's go." and we got in the canoe going upstream. As we were poling the canoe along it began to rain. So we went ashore, we nosed the canoe into the beach at the side stream Miquel and picked some papaya. I got five ripe papaya and put them in the canoe and we continued going upstream. Then there at the mouth of the side stream called Tomás, I shot a *majas* with my shotgun as it was leaving the water after some cat had chased it into the water on the other side of the river. After I shot it, I thought out loud, "Let's go eat it up there ahead." Going, we arrived at the side stream Shanshu, and there in my workhouse where I plant peanuts, we ate it.

Then at 12 o'clock noon I said, "Let's go." We got more turtle eggs as we were going along. Where there were many turtle egg nests, I got three more nests full as we went along. Then there far away I saw an anaconda; the large anaconda, wanting to swallow a *ronsoco,* had caught it. When I saw the anaconda, which had caught a *ronsoco,* I said, "Let's kill it." We tried to kill it but moving away quickly it escaped into the water. As it was escaping into the water, we went on by and continued upstream. Then we slept. After we slept at someone's peanut planting house, we ate fish; we ate *boca chica.*

From there we awoke and moved on. Then I slept at the side stream Dos Amigos. After I got turtle eggs as we traveled along, we slept at Dos Amigos. After we slept we got a fish on a baited hook we had set out overnight. We caught a *sungaro* on a hook, boiled it, ate it, and moved on. Getting turtle eggs as we went along, I dug up one nest at one place, I dug up two nests at another place repeatedly as we traveled along. There far upriver we bypassed Conta and ate at the beach by the side stream that had an old tree covered with vegetation. We boiled twenty turtle eggs. We also boiled a large number of armored fish there. We then ate the fish with boiled cassava.

From there we moved on; then at the mouth of the side stream With Konchmama, I heard a herd of large peccary. As the large peccary were coming, I heard them at 5 o'clock in the afternoon and said, "Let's go shoot them." We went; I was trying to be the first to shoot when I did something to scare them (which I still wonder about) and while they were running away squealing, only my nephew shot one of them. Then I gutted it, took it and loaded it into the canoe. We slept at that same place. In the morning we awoke and I skinned the peccary, cut the meat into strips, salted it, and then we left.

At that same place I was thinking. There I thought, "Good. We are going in the direction of where there are no people," and fell asleep. I awoke in the middle of the night and spoke with God. After I spoke with God, things were good and we again went on. Continually going, then there far away at the mouth of the side stream With Cetico Trees I slept. Before we slept, I said, "Let's now go and cause a large fish to swallow a hook and catch it." We went up the side stream With Cetico Trees. I caught two *mexku* fish and three armored fish. But I did not get any with a hook because the piranha were biting the bait and escaping with it. There I fell asleep and awoke and again talked with God. After I talked with God, I said to them, "Let's go. Maybe the *Maxiku* are coming. Everybody get up so we can travel on. If we do not go at dawn, we may meet them."

In order to go, we got in the canoe at about 9 o'clock and were going. There at a long straight stretch of river we were poling, going along. Then where I shot food with Ken for the *kacha* ceremony and slept long ago, where the current is slow, we were traveling along on a long bend in the river around a large sand bar. We were rounding another large bend and looking up along a long straight stretch of river. Then my son and my grandson were talking a lot and I prohibited them. I said, "Don't talk. If we don't talk, we may see game animals and people approaching before they see us!" After I said that to them, they stopped talking as we traveled along. We were poling along at a beach where someone cut the head off a turtle long ago, where the river took away a lake; we were going out around a large high beach which hid whatever was behind it and I was sitting there in a dream-like state. Then many people were coming, real bodies holding many bows and arrows were coming. A different people were surprised; on our side also we were surprised.

I said, "Don't be afraid! These are the ones we have heard about. Our people always see their footprints and their campsites with fire and temporary vine hammocks. We have met them. They have encountered us today and we have encountered them today so that we may contact and talk with them." I saw them at that same place the other day.

While I was looking at them at that same place, many men were coming toward us with their arrows laid on their bows but not drawn. They all stood upright to look at us and then they all quickly raised their bows and arrows into the air with raised arms the other day. They completely raised their weapons.

We thought, "Oh, they are fierce!" And I said, "Even though they are angry, let's not be afraid. God can do the very difficult. Thus you may see; we may speak with them peaceably." As we kept going in our canoe, they retreated following the long beach. Then I said, "Go over on the other side by the hard clay, while following them. Take the canoe over there." As they continued to retreat, we were going along following, and I said, "They might shoot at us. However, we can also shoot a few times. Let's load our guns." So we loaded the shotguns. After we loaded two shotguns, we continued going, watching them. And then where the beach ended, they were wading across to another beach and we again saw them, lots and lots of them. Not a few, like a whole community maybe. I wonder how many people there were. I wonder if it was fifty real men that we saw the other day. That number of bodies we were not able to take in with our eyes. There was a very great quantity of them.

Then I said to those with me, "What are they like maybe? Maybe their words are like our words. Maybe they are real Yaminahuas. If they are real Yaminahuas, will we be able to understand their words? We always talk with the other Yaminahua at this time. I intend to call to them so we may hear their words. Listen for their words all of you!" Then I called to them; those with me cried out "Hi" with me. I called, "Hi, you all come," and also called them with my hat. "Come! Get this!" I called to them and all those with me cried out, " Hi, Hi, Hi, Hi" the other day. As they were doing that, I said, "To find out how many real men there are, let's follow them."

Wow! That very great quantity ran; that amount climbed the riverbank as I continued to follow. Finally, a group of those whom I had followed stopped in the river. I had followed twelve real men. I was wondering if the other amount, who had run away, were running past us on the high ground while those twelve real men only stayed in the river to trick us while the others got behind us.

They stood in a group and talked to me the other day. Three times I spoke to them the other day. I called, "Hi, Hi, Hi, Hi, Hi, Hi! You all come! We not kill you! You all come! You all come!" In that way I called to them and they did the same to me, however, I did not understand their words. Maybe they were thinking that I was speaking badly. Whatever they said, I do not know. While they were calling to me, I called back to them the other day. "Come! Come! Come, so we may talk! Come, so we may talk!" I did that not understanding them the other day.

Thus, I thought and was afraid of those who had run with their bows and arrows. Then I said, "Ahh, why am I doing this? Let's go, they can shoot us." I said that to my nephew. Then I thought and said, "Okay. Wait a little while. My thinking is again good. Let's leave some things for them as we go away, so that we can contact them peaceably in the future and report that to our people. A bowl maybe, or my clothing maybe, or whatever we can leave for them." However, we felt compassion for our things and wanted to keep them. I was the only one who wanted to leave my two things, two plastic bags, one black, the other red, and my drinking container made from a tin can.

With that being the situation, I drove a cane pole into the sand, standing it upright and then I attached the things to the top. I split the pole and hung the bags in the slit. Then I again called to them, "Hi, Hi, Hi. Come to get! Come to get!" Then I said to those in the canoe, "Go, they may have bypassed us by this time. They could shoot us." Turning the canoe around we started downstream and got it stuck on a sunken log in the shallow water. I said, "We have stuck the canoe on a sunken log. Let's get it off, they are coming." So we got down out of the canoe and finally pushed it free. And while we were poling, coming in this direction, they came running on the beach. They passed us running and jumped into the river the other day. When they jumped in the water, we said, "Now they may be coming to call us. Or maybe they are coming to get the things we left for them today. Let's watch for the time being."

They did not take the things we hung on the pole for them. They came running past them with their bows and arrows, jumped into the water, climbed out on another beach and came running. They came running, covering their genitals with one hand or maybe with their penises flopping. Maybe they work that way. Holding their genitals they came running furiously; two of them came running furiously. Then about the distance to that tree over there [about 40 meters] they stopped on a large beach sandbar. One of them put his arrows between his legs and drew an arrow on his bow pointed at us the other day.

My nephew said, "He is shooting at us. Shoot him!"

But I said, "Let's not touch them." And even though he had drawn an arrow, I again called to them, "Take this hat! Don't shoot at us! Take this hat!" He did not listen to what I said and discharged an arrow in our direction. The arrow was coming and approached very close to us; about as far as from me to that door [6 meters], it hit the sand. Its bamboo point broke when it hit.

I said, "Okay. Let's go without getting the arrow. He wants to shoot us. Shoot into the air. With his arrow he scared us today; let's scare them also!" Then we fired our shotguns; we fired our shotguns upwards four times. "Tu, Tu, Tu, Tu," we did and while they were running away, we poled and poled behind their backs. Then I said, "Maybe they crossed over to this loop in the river and are again hidden here. Fire off a shot here!" He fired. Then at a place where there were lots of vines growing close to the river, I said, "At a place like this they always hide!" He again fired off a shot. From there again poling, coming continually poling, with fear we were coming. With fear only we were coming in this direction; we bypassed the mouth of the side stream With Cetico Trees, where we slept a few days ago. Even though we were thinking in vain that they were coming, we kept coming anyways; I was filled with fear. Coming in this direction, we bypassed the place where we shot the large peccary and slept several days ago and kept right on coming in this direction.

Filomeno and his crew returned to Santa Rey, and I quickly received exaggerated reports of their encounter. So I sent word and invited Filomeno, who had been my next-door neighbor in Balta for many years, to come and tell me his story directly.

Filomeno's rapid decision to make this trip to collect turtle eggs was not at all unusual. He probably made a quick decision to avoid its becoming a large expedition. The Cashinahua relish the rich taste of these small leathery shelled eggs, because most of their game meat is very lean and they want the taste of fat in their diet. They made quick stops at gardens they had on high spots along the river to collect food. The cooking bananas are always cut green and would easily last the time they were away. The cassava tubers are the nonpoisonous sweet variety which do not keep as long as the bananas, so were boiled or roasted first. Hunting or fishing for their meat is normal on most of their trips, and they salted the peccary meat to take home to their families along with most of the turtle eggs. Poling is the norm for traveling far upriver during the dry season. They still have a few motors but those need a larger canoe, which would be impractical in the shallow water. Also gasoline is far too expensive for such a trip; it costs about two days' wages to buy a gallon. The motors are used on the larger canoes to make the four- to five-day round trip to Puerto Esperanza.

All the beaches upstream for two or three days' poling distance are used to grow peanuts during the dry season (late May to October). Peanuts are also planted in the well-drained hillside gardens to augment their major summer crop. Back in the early 1970s when they were hunting for skins and occasionally collecting rubber, they built more substantial houses and planted small gardens of cassava and bananas near the beaches they claimed as peanut gardens so that they could take their families for several weeks. This enabled them to carry on the commercial activities in more remote areas, increasing their chances of success. Now in the 1990s the upriver areas serve only as areas to plant peanuts, hunt for meat, and collect turtle eggs.

With the reduction in population, rubber collecting, and commercial hunting, the area upstream from Balta has become wilder. In 1994 I saw more anacondas on the beaches around Balta than we saw when we lived there. The anaconda was not hunted commercially or for food, but Cashinahua men will kill them when they think they are a threat. I saw one killed at Balta in 1971 because it was eating their domesticated ducks. The other large aquatic animal they fear is the large caiman, often called an alligator. I saw a 14-foot caiman in 1970, but by the mid-1970s the vast majority had been turned into shoes and handbags. However, I believe there are breeding adult caiman living at the headwaters and far up the side streams flowing into the Curanja River. In about 1978, on a long hike up the side stream Balta, we found a caiman nest mound. The men were very agitated and looked all around to make sure that the female was not guarding the nest. They then dug it open and removed the large, almost spherical eggs to be eaten later. It is their custom to take all the eggs in a caiman or turtle nest and when hunting to kill as many of the peccary in a herd as they can, but sparing the lead sow so that the herd will continue to migrate past their village.

In their entire cultural history there has always been more land than they could possibly use, more game animals than they could possibly shoot, and more turtle eggs than they could possibly collect. They always had the luxury of abundant natural resources. But by meeting the Mashku-Piro they are now mentally boxed in. Even though they have been drifting slowly closer to the world of the outsiders, they have always had the wilderness upstream as a place to escape to if necessary, much as their grandparents had in Brazil. They now feel threatened by the existence of these long-rumored Mashku-Piro and one of the matriarchs of Balta emphatically asked me to get on my radio to tell the Peruvian military to "Bomb those *bravos* (wild ones) who were on their river."

The name "Mashku-Piro" is a guess, because those who have heard them speak say it does not sound like a Panoan or Arawakan language. The best guess is that they are related to the Piro, who live in the Ucayali Valley. There have been sightings for some thirty years of a nomadic hunter-gatherer group living in the high jungle periphery of the Alto Purús region. They have always been elusive and passive, but not ignorant of the outside world. The contact on the upper Curanja, however, was different. Filomeno and his men would have appeared to them as Peruvians because of their dress, but this was the first time I have heard of them shooting an arrow at anyone. This may not even have been the group whom people have intermittently seen for years but a different one, who have moved in from the Juruá drainage to the north.

Whoever they are, I have been receiving letters for the past three years from my Cashinahua friends saying that those people have come down the Curanja River and are stealing from their gardens. This has especially affected those who live in Santa Rey, which is now the farthest village upriver. The Cashinahua continually see footprints in their gardens, and some of their crops are gone. They say they are afraid these people will come and steal everything they have. When Filomeno said, "We had compassion for our things," while they were deciding what they would leave for the people they had encountered, he was really saying, "We care for our things the way we care for our children."

The Cashinahua of Peru have worked long and hard to gain the things they know their parents lacked, and now feel threatened beause they never see those who are stealing from their gardens. This is ironic, because they all know the stories about their ancestors stealing their first chickens and banana plants from other indigenous groups' gardens, and now they find themselves on the reverse side of the story.

This study has documented an important transition for the Cashinahua of Peru, from isolation to an existence on the edge of two dominant cultures. This series of narratives from the past to the present indicates how the Cashinahua's past has influenced their cautious approach to the outside world, and details their activities as they participate in the shaping of their own future. They want to gain their living from the rain forest and to obtain as much as possible from the outside world as well.

The Cashinahua have emerged as the largest block of voters in the Purús province and are presently considering how they might use this unfamiliar position. They can easily influence elections in favor of a candidate who is friendly to their interests. One Cashinahua friend who had the education and ability to occupy the position as head of the frontier province told me it was better to have a Peruvian outsider handle the headaches of dealing with Lima. This is a continuation of their past preference to have a go-between deal with the outside world. And there was another reason paramount in his thinking. The mayor of Puerto Esperanza had recently been shot and wounded in the city of Pucallpa as he emerged from a bank.

This highlights an unchanged point in their thinking. Even though they have changed their mode of dress, have personal documents and have learned to interface with the outsiders, they do not identify themselves as Peruvians. To them, Peruvians are outsiders. They still consider themselves to be the Genuine people because they have Genuine names, Genuine relatives, and speak the Genuine language. Just as their ancestors who worked for rubber collectors and dressed in rubber-collector clothes remained Genuine people, they also remain the Genuine people. Clothing may facilitate contact, but as long as they live in villages separate from the outsiders and gain their living from the rain forest, the Cashinahua will basically remain the same, even though they are slowly changing. However, Grompes did register doubt when he told me that if the outsiders continue to take their best students to Pucallpa and Lima for further education, they will one by one change all of his people into outsiders.

Many anthropologists believe that the intervention by missionaries on behalf of indigenous people is subtly preparing them for destruction of their culture (Comaroff 1992:161; Stoll 1982). Representatives of any outsider cultures function as agents of cultural change. Cultural survival for the Cashinahua (and any indigenous people) is possible if they are allowed to adapt in their own way and at their own pace to the outside world. Cultural survival does not mean preserving traditional society, but rather permitting a group to successfully adapt to change.

I have seen the Cashinahua adopt many changes so they could remain the same—being the Genuine people. However idealistic the above may be, the Cashinahua did not choose the timing of their being influenced or impinged upon by other cultures. The Cashinahua's history and past social contexts demonstrate that other spiritual beliefs came to them prior to the arrival of Europeans. The names "God" and "Jesus" came with the invaders. Our translation of the New Testament gave them a source text to help them understand and decide for themselves concerning what people have been telling them.

The extent of our influence on them is difficult for us to evaluate objectively. I think the Cashinahua of Peru count me as a true friend, but I also found out where I fit into their world during one of my visits. In 1985 when I asked Grompes, during a candid talk one day, "What did you all think of me when I first got off the airplane long ago?" he looked at me with a little grin and said, "We thought, 'What can we get out of him.'" I would like to see my Cashinahua friends have the material progress they want and maintain their identity while becoming bicultural—interacting with the national culture when necessary, yet retaining their own Genuine language and culture.

Appendix:

Map of the Upper Tarauacá River

Adaptation of map by Constant Tastevin from
La Geographie Tome XLV
Janvier–Fevrier 1926
Paris, France

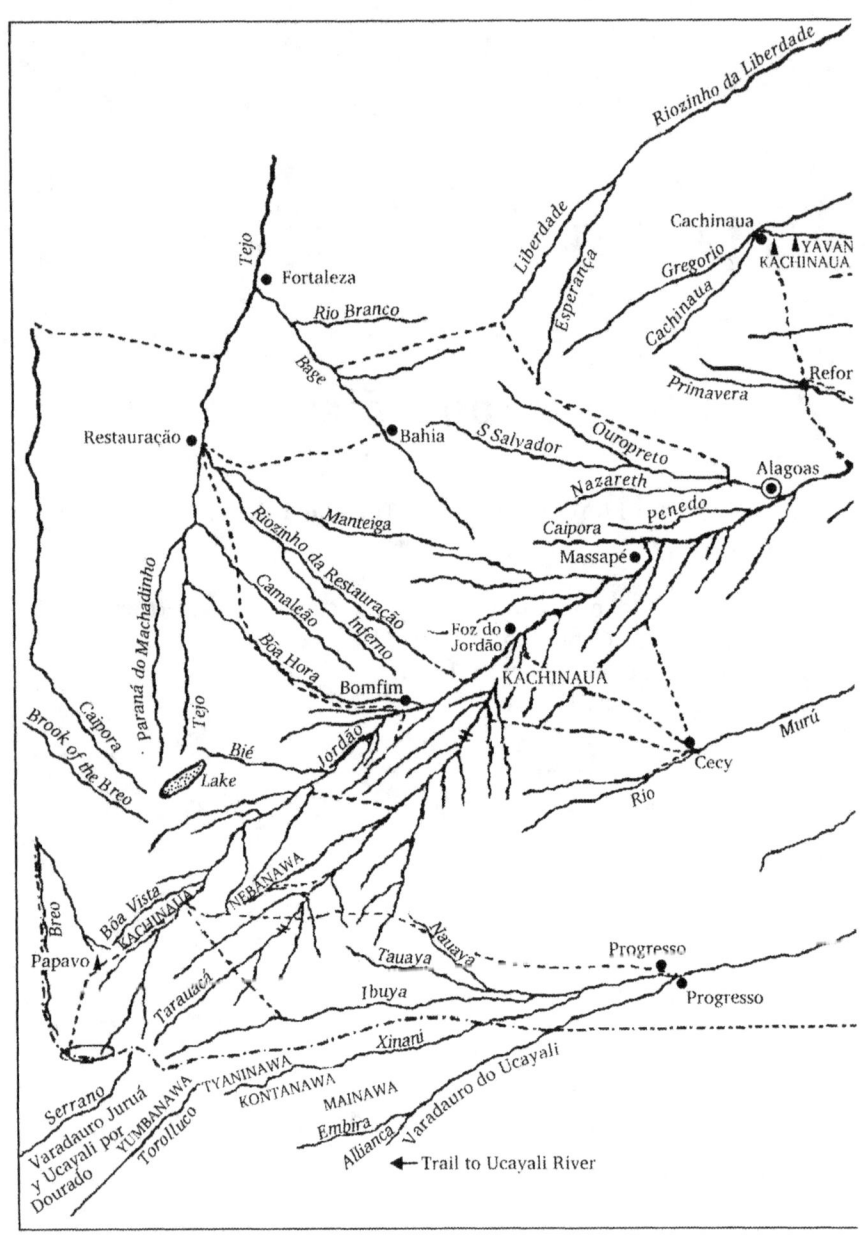

Appendix:

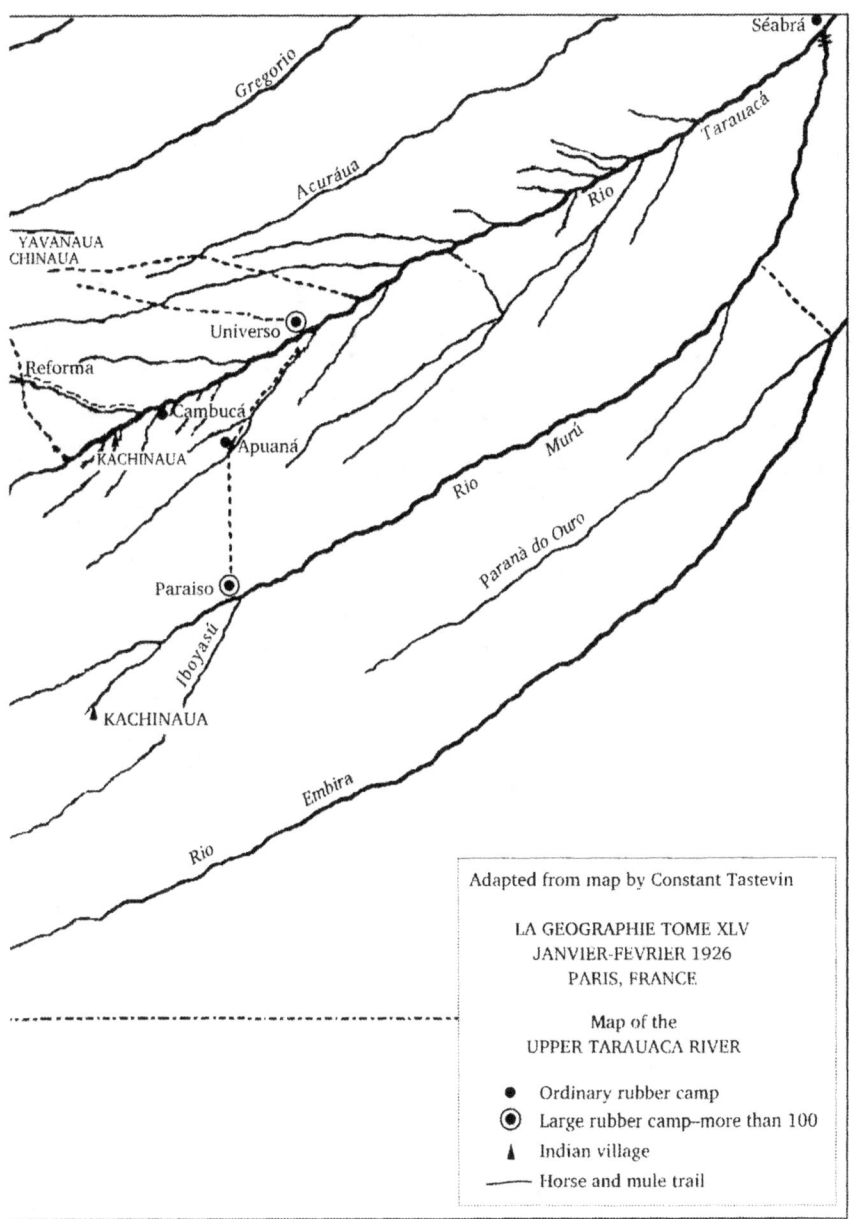

References

Beidelman, Thomas O. 1982. Colonial evangelism. Bloomington: Indiana University Press.

Capistrano de Abreu, J. 1911. Os Caxinauás: Dois Depoimentos. Rio de Janeiro, Jornal do Commercio de 25 de Dezembro de 1911 e de 7 e 14 de Janeiro de 1912.

Capistrano de Abreu, J. 1914. *Ra-txa hu-ni-ku-i* Gramatica, Textos e Vocabulario Caxinauás. Rio de Janeiro: Ediçao da Sociedade Capistrano de Abreu.

Chandless, William. 1867. Ascent of the river Purus. Journal of the Royal Geographic Society 35:86–128.

Comaroff, John, and Jean Comaroff. 1992. Ethnography and the historical imagination. Boulder, Colo.: Westview Press.

Dirks, Nicholas B., ed. 1992. Colonialism and culture. Ann Arbor: University of Michigan Press.

Harner, Michael. 1993. Waiting for Inca God: Culture, myth, and history. South American Indian Studies 1:53–60. Bennington, Vt. Bennington College.

Hemming, John. 1978. Red gold. London: MacMillan.

Hemming, John. 1987. Amazon frontier. London: MacMillan.

Kensinger, Kenneth M. 1995. How real people ought to live. Prospect Heights, Ill.: Waveland Press.

Kensinger, Kenneth M. 1998. Unsettled Communities: Changing perspectives. In Debra Picchi (ed.), South American indigenous settlements, 29–32. South American Indian Studies 5. Bennington, Vt.: Bennington College.

Kensinger, Kenneth M, et al. 1975. Studying the Cashinahua. In The Cashinahua of eastern Peru. Providence, R.I: Haffenreffer Museum of Anthropology.
McCallum, Cecilia. 1989. Gender, personhood, and social organization amongst the Cashinahua of western Amazonia. Ph.D. dissertation. London School of Economics, University of London.
Meggers, Betty J. 1971. Amazonia: Man and culture in a counterfeit paradise. Arlington Heights, Ill.: Harlan Davidson.
Price, T. Douglas, and Gary M. Feinman. 1997. Images of the past. Mountain View, Calif.: Mayfield.
Schultz, Harald. 1962. *Hombre*. New York: MacMillan.
Schultz, Harald, and Wilma Chiara. 1955. Informaçoes sôbre os indios do alto rio Purus. Revista do Museu Paulista, IX:181–201. Sao Paulo, Brasil.
Siskind, Janet. 1973. To hunt in the morning. New York: Oxford University Press.
Sombra, Luiz. 1913. Os Cachinauás. Rio de Janeiro: Jornal do Commércio 11 de Janeiro.
Stoll, David. 1982. Fishers of men or founders of empire? The Wycliffe Bible translators in Latin America. London: Zed Press; Cambridge: Culture Survival, Inc.
Stoll, David. 1990. Is Latin America turning Protestant? Berkley: University of California Press.
Tastevin, Constant. 1943. The middle Amazon: Its people and geography. Coordinator of Inter-American Affairs, Washington, D.C.: U.S. Office for Emergency Management.
Williamson, Edwin. 1992. The Penguin history of Latin America. Allen Lane: The Penguin Press.

SIL International and The International Museum of Cultures Publications in Ethnography

Recent Publications

38. **A tale of Pudicho's people,** by Richard Montag. 2002.
37. **African friends and money matters,** by David Maranz, 2001.
36. **The value of the person in the Guahibo culture,** by Marcelino Sosa, Walter del Aguila, trans., 2000.
35. **People of the drum of God—Come!,** by Paul Neeley. 1999.
34. **Cashibo folklore and culture: Prose, poetry, and historical background,** by Lila Wistrand-Robinson, 1998.
33. **Symbolism and ritual in Irian Jaya: A glimpse of seven systems,** by Marilyn Gregerson and Joyce Sterner, eds., 1997.
32. **Kinship and social organization in Irian Jaya,** by Marilyn Gregerson and Joyce Sterner, eds., 1997.
31. **Ritual, belief, and kinship,** by Marilyn Gregerson, ed., 1993.
30. **Rituals and relationships in the Valley of the Sun: The Ketengban of Irian Jaya,** by Andrew Sims and Anne Sims, 1992.
29. Not published.
28. **Peace is everything,** by David E. Maranz, 1993.
27. **Mice are men: Language and society among the Murle of Sudan,** by Jonathon E. Arensen, 1992.
26. **Language choice in rural development,** by Clinton D. W. Robinson, 1992.
25. **El arte cofan en tejido de hamacas. The Cofan art of hammock weaving,** by M. B. Borman, 1992.
24. **Development program planning: A process approach,** by David Spaeth, 1991.
23. **Nucleation in Papua New Guinea cultures,** by Marvin K. Mayers and Daniel D. Rath, eds., 1987.
22. **Current concerns of anthropologists and missionaries,** by Karl Franklin, ed., 1987.
21. **Tales from Indochina,** by Marilyn Gregerson, Dorothy Thomas, Doris Blood, and Carol Zylstra, eds., 1987.
20. **The formal content of ethnography,** by Philip K. Bock, 1986.
19. **Five Amazonian studies on world view and cultural change,** by William R. Merrifield, ed., 1985.

For further information or a full listing of SIL publications contact:

International Academic Bookstore
Summer Institute of Linguistics
7500 W. Camp Wisdom Road
Dallas, TX 75236-5699

Voice: 972-708-7404
Fax: 972-708-7363
Email: academic.books@sil.org
Internet: http://www.ethnologue.com

www.ingramcontent.com/pod-product-compliance
Lightning Source LLC
Chambersburg PA
CBHW060955230426
43665CB00015B/2206